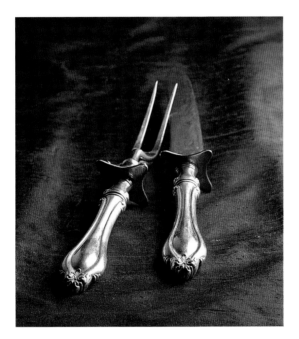

WILLIAMS-SONOMA

THANKSGIVING

RECIPES AND TEXT
MICHAEL McLAUGHLIN

GENERAL EDITOR
CHUCK WILLIAMS

PHOTOGRAPHS
NOEL BARNHURST

SIMON & SCHUSTER • SOURCE
NEW YORK • LONDON • TORONTO • SYDNEY • SINGAPORE

CONTENTS

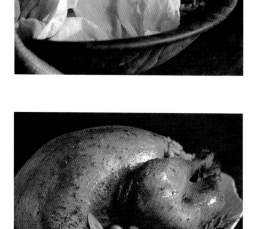

VEGETABLES AND RELISHES

POTATOES ON THE SIDE

DESSERTS

INTRODUCTION

For the novice cook, being faced with the challenge of preparing an entire Thanksgiving dinner can be overwhelming. So many of our meals now are quick and convenient, but Thanksgiving is all about traditions, including the tradition of old-fashioned home cooking. This cookbook is intended to help the new cook, and to be a source of inspiration to the more experienced one.

Before you do anything else, turn to the Basics chapter on page 109. There you'll find helpful instructions about choosing a menu, preparing a turkey, and planning the cooking. Then, once you've decided on the recipes for each course, read through them all ahead of time, paying attention to the make-ahead tips that will help you organize your time. With a little forethought, a daunting task can be transformed into a satisfying experience in the kitchen. Whether this is your first time preparing the Thanksgiving meal or your twentieth, I hope these recipes make your feast a memorable and enjoyable one.

Chuck Williams

STARTERS, SALADS, AND SOUPS

Whether it is offered as a stand-up nibble or served formally at the table, a Thanksgiving first course may well present the cook's most creative challenge in putting together the menu.

CURRIED NUTS AND RAISINS

Position a rack in the upper third of the oven and preheat to 375°F (190°C). Lightly but evenly coat a shallow baking pan with vegetable oil.

In a small bowl, mix together the curry powder, black pepper, ginger, salt, sugar, white pepper, cayenne, and cinnamon.

In a large bowl, beat the egg whites until blended but not foamy. Add the cashews, peanuts, sunflower seeds, and sesame seeds and stir to coat them evenly. Immediately sprinkle the spice mixture over the nuts, again stirring to coat evenly.

Spread the nut mixture in an even layer in the prepared baking pan. Transfer to the oven and bake for 5 minutes. Stir the nuts to break up any clumps. Continue to bake, stirring once or twice, until the nuts are crisp, dry, and fragrant, 10–12 minutes. Place the pan on a wire rack and let the nuts cool completely.

Transfer the mixture to an airtight container and let stand at room temperature for 24 hours to develop the flavors. Stir the raisins into the nuts just before serving.

Make-Ahead Tip: The nuts must be made 24 hours ahead of serving and can be prepared up to 3 days in advance (or even a day or 2 longer in dry weather). If they get a little soft, reheat them on a baking sheet in a preheated 300°F (150°C) oven until crisp, about 10 minutes. Add the raisins at the last minute, or their moisture will make the nuts soggy.

MAKES 8–10 SERVINGS

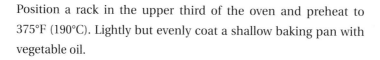

CURRY POWDER

Brands of curry powder are as distinctively different from one another as chili powders. Choose one that suits your palate and the dish you are preparing. For best results in this recipe, select a reddish brown type, with a mellow fragrance and a medium heat level. A bright yellow curry, heavy with turmeric flavor, would overpower the dish.

Vegetable oil or oil spray for coating

2 tablespoons curry powder

1 teaspoon freshly ground black pepper

¾ teaspoon ground ginger

½ teaspoon salt

½ teaspoon sugar

¼ teaspoon freshly ground white pepper

¼ teaspoon cayenne pepper

⅛ teaspoon ground cinnamon

2 egg whites, at room temperature

1½ cups (8 oz/250 g) salted roasted cashews

⅔ cup (4 oz/125 g) salted roasted peanuts

1 cup (4 oz/125 g) shelled sunflower seeds

¼ cup (1¼ oz/37 g) sesame seeds

1 cup (6 oz/185 g) raisins

SPICY THREE-CHEESE SPREAD

6 oz (185 g) aged Swiss or Gruyère cheese, at room temperature

6 oz (185 g) sharp orange Cheddar cheese, at room temperature

4 oz (125 g) mild, creamy blue cheese such as Maytag, at room temperature

6 tablespoons (3 oz/90 g) unsalted butter, at room temperature

⅓ cup (3 fl oz/80 ml) young tawny Port *(far right)*

4 teaspoons Dijon mustard

¾ teaspoon hot-pepper sauce such as Tabasco

Salt and freshly ground pepper

1 green (spring) onion, including tender green parts, finely chopped

FOR THE TOASTS:

About 30 thin baguette slices

⅓ cup (3 fl oz/80 ml) olive oil

Cut the Swiss and Cheddar cheeses into ½-inch (12-mm) cubes. Crumble the blue cheese. In a food processor, combine the 3 cheeses, butter, Port, mustard, hot-pepper sauce, ½ teaspoon salt, and ½ teaspoon pepper. Process, stopping several times and scraping down the sides of the work bowl, until smooth. Transfer to a bowl and stir in the green onion. Cover and refrigerate for at least 24 hours to develop the flavors.

To make the toasts, position oven racks in the upper and lower thirds of the oven and preheat to 400°F (200°C). Brush the baguette slices on one side only with the oil. Arrange the slices, oil side up, on 2 baking sheets. Transfer the sheets to the oven and bake until lightly colored but still a little soft, about 7 minutes total, switching the top and bottom pans halfway through baking. Place the pans on a wire rack and let the toasts cool to room temperature. They will crisp further as they cool.

To serve, let the cheese spread sit at room temperature until slightly softened, then transfer to a decorative serving dish. Serve accompanied with the toasts.

Make-Ahead Tip: The cheese spread must be made at least 24 hours in advance and can be made up to 3 days ahead. The toasts can be baked early in the day. When cool, store them at room temperature in an airtight container.

MAKES 8–10 SERVINGS

PORT STYLES

Originally from Portugal's Douro region, Port is a fortified wine produced by adding high-strength grape alcohol to wine, stopping the fermentation process, and leaving the wine with a residual sweetness. Unblended vintage Port is bottled after two years in wood barrels; it continues to age in the bottle. Other Ports, including tawny Port, are blended and aged in wood. The less-complex young tawny Port called for in this recipe mellows the sharp flavors of the cheeses with a touch of sweetness.

CRUDITÉS WITH
HONEY-MUSTARD DIP

Line a fine-mesh sieve with cheesecloth (muslin) and place over a bowl. Spoon the yogurt into the sieve and let it drain at room temperature, stirring it once or twice, for 2 hours.

In a bowl, combine the drained yogurt, mustard, dill, ½ teaspoon salt, and ½ teaspoon pepper. Mix well, cover, and refrigerate for at least 24 hours to develop the flavors.

Close to serving, cut the vegetables into narrow strips 5 inches (13 cm) long. Adjust the dip's seasoning with salt and pepper to taste. Transfer to a decorative bowl and serve with the vegetables for dipping.

Make-Ahead Tip: The dip must be made at least 24 hours in advance and can be completed up to 3 days ahead.

MAKES 8–10 SERVINGS

2 cups (1 lb/500 g) plain yogurt

⅔ cup (5 oz/155 g) honey Dijon mustard

⅓ cup (½ oz/15 g) minced fresh dill

Salt and freshly ground pepper

About 2 lb (1 kg) assorted raw vegetables such as bell peppers (capsicums), carrots, fennel, and celery

VEGETABLE VARIATION

If you want to supplement the raw vegetables in this dish with some lightly cooked ones, good choices would be green beans, broccoli, sugar snap peas, and cauliflower. To prepare, bring a pot of water to a boil, salt it lightly, and add the trimmed or cut-up vegetables. Cook, stirring occasionally, until the vegetables are crisp-tender, about 5 minutes. Drain and immerse in a bowl of ice water for about 1 minute to stop the cooking and set the color. Drain again and pat dry.

MUSHROOMS STUFFED WITH CRAB AND ALMONDS

⅓ cup (2 oz/60 g) unblanched almonds

¼ cup (2 oz/60 g) unsalted butter, plus extra for greasing

24 large fresh cremini or white mushrooms, about 3 lb (1.5 kg) total weight, brushed clean and stems removed and reserved

½ cup (2½ oz/75 g) finely chopped red bell pepper (capsicum)

1½ teaspoons minced fresh thyme or ½ teaspoon dried

2 cloves garlic, minced

Salt and freshly ground pepper

1½ cups (3 oz/90 g) coarse fresh bread crumbs *(far right)*

1 cup (6 oz/185 g) fresh lump crabmeat, picked over for shell fragments

⅓ cup (3 fl oz/80 ml) canned low-sodium chicken broth

2 eggs, beaten

⅓ cup (⅓ oz/10 g) minced fresh flat-leaf (Italian) parsley

¾ cup (6 fl oz/180 ml) dry white wine

Position a rack in the upper third of the oven and preheat to 400°F (200°C). Pour the almonds into a shallow metal pan and toast in the oven, stirring once or twice, until crisp and fragrant, about 10 minutes. Let cool and coarsely chop.

Raise the oven temperature to 450°F (230°C). Generously grease two 9-by-13-inch (23-by-33-cm) baking dishes with butter.

In a food processor, finely chop the mushroom stems. In a frying pan over medium heat, melt the ¼ cup butter. Add the bell pepper, thyme, and garlic, cover, and cook, stirring occasionally, until softened, about 5 minutes. Add the mushroom stems and ½ teaspoon salt. Cover and cook, stirring occasionally, for 4 minutes. Raise the heat to high, uncover, and cook, stirring often, until the mixture is dry and lightly browned, about 2 minutes. Set aside and let cool.

In a large bowl, gently toss together the almonds, mushroom stem mixture, bread crumbs, and crabmeat. Add the broth, eggs, parsley, ½ teaspoon salt, and pepper to taste, then toss again. Mound the crab mixture in the mushroom caps, dividing it evenly. Arrange the mushrooms in the baking dishes. Drizzle with the wine.

Place both dishes on the oven's upper rack and bake until the mushrooms are tender and the stuffing lightly browned, about 15 minutes; rotate the dishes halfway through baking and baste the mushrooms with the pan juices. Remove the mushrooms from the oven and let rest in their dishes for 5 minutes. Serve hot.

Make-Ahead Tip: The stuffing should be prepared just before serving, but the crab can be picked over and the mushroom stems sautéed several hours in advance.

MAKES 8–10 SERVINGS

FRESH BREAD CRUMBS
Coarse fresh bread crumbs keep this mushroom stuffing moist and light. To make fresh crumbs, choose a firm, white coarse country loaf, sliced or not, about 3 days old. Avoid overly sweet breads or very tart sour-doughs. Trim off the crusts, cut the bread into 2-inch (5-cm) cubes, and pulse in a food processor to make coarse crumbs. Freeze any leftover crumbs and use them within 1 month.

BUTTERNUT SQUASH SOUP

Preheat the oven to 450°F (230°C). In a small bowl, stir together the honey and oil. Line a shallow baking dish with aluminum foil and arrange the squashes, onions, and apple in it. Brush the cut sides of the squash halves and the entire surface of the onions and apple with the honey mixture. Bake, turning all the pieces once or twice, until tender and well browned, about 1 hour. Remove from the oven, let cool, and then scoop the squash flesh out of the peel and chop coarsely. Chop the onions and apple.

In a soup pot over medium heat, combine the squash, onion, apple, stock, ½ teaspoon salt, ½ teaspoon pepper, and the nutmeg. Bring to a simmer over medium heat. Partially cover and cook until very tender, about 20 minutes. Remove from the heat and let cool.

In a blender or food processor, purée the soup in batches until smooth. Return the soup to the pot and place over medium heat. Stir in the half-and-half and bring to a simmer. Taste and adjust the seasoning with salt and pepper.

Divide the soup among warmed shallow serving bowls. Evenly sprinkle each portion with the pistachios and sage and serve immediately.

Make-Ahead Tip: The soup can be prepared through the addition of the half-and-half up to 2 days in advance. To serve, reheat, taste and adjust the seasoning, and garnish.

MAKES 8 SERVINGS

CARAMELIZING

Sugar may be caramelized, but so can sweet fruits and vegetables. As the squashes, onions, and apple in this recipe roast in the oven, the sugars naturally present in them slowly develop a golden brown color and a less purely sweet, more complex flavor through long cooking. Adding a sprinkling of sugar or, as seen here, a brushing of honey, encourages the caramelizing process.

2 tablespoons honey

3 tablespoons canola or other light vegetable oil

2 butternut squashes, about 3 lb (1.5 kg) total weight, halved lengthwise and seeded

2 yellow onions, quartered

1 Granny Smith apple, peeled, quartered, and cored

5 cups (40 fl oz/1.25 l) chicken stock or canned low-sodium chicken broth

Salt and freshly ground pepper

¼ teaspoon freshly grated nutmeg

½ cup (4 fl oz/125 ml) half-and-half (half cream)

⅓ cup (1½ oz/45 g) coarsely chopped pistachios

4 teaspoons minced fresh sage

SHERRIED SHRIMP BISQUE

¼ cup (2 oz/60 g) unsalted butter

2 lb (1 kg) small shrimp (prawns), peeled and deveined (page 123), shells reserved

1¼ cups (6 oz/185 g) finely chopped carrot

½ cup (2½ oz/75 g) finely chopped celery

½ cup (2½ oz/75 g) finely chopped shallot

1 teaspoon finely chopped fresh thyme, plus extra for garnish, or ¼ teaspoon dried

2 tablespoons unbleached all-purpose (plain) flour

4 cups (32 fl oz/1 l) chicken stock or low-sodium canned chicken broth

¾ cup (6 fl oz/180 ml) medium-dry sherry

1 can (14½ oz/455 g) crushed tomatoes with purée

½ cup (4 fl oz/125 ml) heavy (double) cream

2 egg yolks

Salt and freshly ground pepper

In a nonaluminum saucepan over low heat, melt the butter. Add the shrimp shells, carrot, celery, shallot, and 1 teaspoon fresh or ¼ teaspoon dried thyme. Cover and cook, stirring once or twice, until the vegetables are softened and the mixture is fragrant, about 10 minutes. Uncover the pan, sprinkle the flour over the shell mixture, and cook uncovered, stirring once or twice, for 2 minutes. Do not allow the mixture to brown. Gradually stir in the stock and sherry. Bring to a simmer, cover partially, and cook, stirring occasionally, for 15 minutes to blend the flavors. Pour the mixture through a sieve set over a bowl and press hard with the back of a spoon to extract all the liquid from the solids. There should be 4 cups (32 fl oz/1 l) liquid. Discard the solids.

Wipe the pan clean, return the strained liquid to it, and set over medium-low heat. Stir in the shrimp and the tomatoes with their purée. In a small bowl, thoroughly whisk together the cream and egg yolks. Stir the cream mixture, ¾ teaspoon salt, and ½ teaspoon pepper into the pan. Cook, stirring often, until the soup is steaming and thickened and the shrimp are pink, curled, and just cooked through, 10–12 minutes. Do not allow the mixture to boil. Taste and adjust the seasoning with salt and pepper.

Ladle the soup into warmed shallow serving bowls, garnish with fresh thyme (if using), and serve immediately.

Make-Ahead Tip: This soup can be prepared through the step of straining the liquid base up to 1 day ahead. Let cool, cover, and refrigerate, returning it to room temperature before proceeding.

MAKES 8 SERVINGS

SHERRY

This famous fortified wine of southwestern Spain, made from the Palomino Fino grape, comes in eight different types, distinguished primarily by color, flavor, sweetness, and alcohol content. The best known of these are pale gold, dry *fino;* very pale and very dry *manzanilla;* darker, slightly nutty tasting, and dry to medium-dry *amontillado;* and mahogany brown, highly aromatic, sweet cream sherry. *Amontillado* would be a good selection for this dish.

WATERCRESS, ENDIVE, AND PEAR SALAD

HAZELNUTS

Also known as filberts, hazelnuts are small, spherical nuts with a sweet, rich, robust flavor, never so welcome as in autumn. They have hard shells that are difficult to crack and are usually sold already shelled. Toasting not only develops the flavor, but also helps the cook remove the nut's tough skin, which can be bitter. Hazelnuts make one of the most assertive nut oils, which adds a pleasant depth of flavor to green salads. Once opened, refrigerate the oil to maintain freshness.

Preheat the oven to 375°F (190°C). In a shallow metal pan, toast the hazelnuts, stirring once or twice, until crisp, fragrant, and brown, about 10 minutes. Wrap the hot nuts in a clean kitchen towel and let steam for 1 minute, then vigorously roll the wrapped nuts between the palms of your hands until most of the dark brown skins are removed. Pick the nuts out of the debris of the peels and coarsely chop them.

In a large bowl, toss together the watercress and endive. Drizzle with the oil and toss again. Sprinkle ½ teaspoon salt over the greens and toss again. Add the hazelnuts, vinegar, and ½ teaspoon pepper and toss well. Taste and adjust the seasoning.

Divide the greens among individual plates. Halve and core the pears and cut each half lengthwise into eighths. Garnish each plate with wedges of pear, tucking them into the greens. Serve immediately.

Make-Ahead Tip: The nuts can be toasted and skinned 1 day ahead; store in an airtight jar at room temperature. Chop them shortly before completing the salad.

MAKES 8-10 SERVINGS

⅔ cup (3½ oz/105 g) hazelnuts (filberts)

3 large bunches watercress, about 1½ lb (750 g) total weight, tough stems removed

3 heads Belgian endive (chicory/witloof), about 1 lb (500 g) total weight, cored and separated into leaves

5 tablespoons (3 fl oz/ 80 ml) hazelnut oil or extra-virgin olive oil

Salt and freshly ground pepper

3 tablespoons pear vinegar or white balsamic vinegar

3 small, ripe but firm pears, preferably red Bartlett (Williams')

MIXED GREENS WITH BACON-WRAPPED FIGS

16 large, plump figs, preferably Black Mission, fresh or dried

8 slices smoked bacon (not thick-cut), halved crosswise

1 lb (500 g) mixed young tender salad greens

⅓ cup (3 fl oz/80 ml) extra-virgin olive oil

Salt and freshly ground pepper

3½ tablespoons sherry vinegar

½ lb (250 g) Stilton cheese, at room temperature

Wrap each fig in a half slice of bacon, overlapping it as necessary and securing it with a toothpick.

Heat a large nonstick frying pan over medium heat. Add the figs and cook, turning occasionally, until the bacon is browned and crisp on all but one side. Remove the toothpicks and turn the figs to finish browning the bacon on all sides. Transfer to a plate and keep warm.

In a very large bowl, toss the greens with the oil. Add ½ teaspoon salt and toss again. Add the vinegar and toss. Add the cheese, crumbling it between your fingers. Season generously with pepper and toss again.

Divide the greens among individual plates. Place 2 figs on each plate. Season the figs with pepper and serve.

Serving Tip: To serve 10 people, keep the greens, cheese, and dressing quantities as given and add 4 more bacon-wrapped figs.

Make-Ahead Tip: The figs should be browned and the salad dressed at the last minute, but the fruit can be wrapped in bacon several hours in advance. Loosely cover the figs and refrigerate, letting them return to room temperature before proceeding.

MAKES 8 SERVINGS

STILTON CHEESE

English Stilton is one of the world's great cheeses, richly flavored and satisfying. Its dense texture and creamy white to ivory color are enhanced by a blue-green veining, created by a special strain of mold. Most Stiltons are now factory produced, but a few manufacturers still make and tend the wheels by hand. For the best quality, seek out these premium examples.

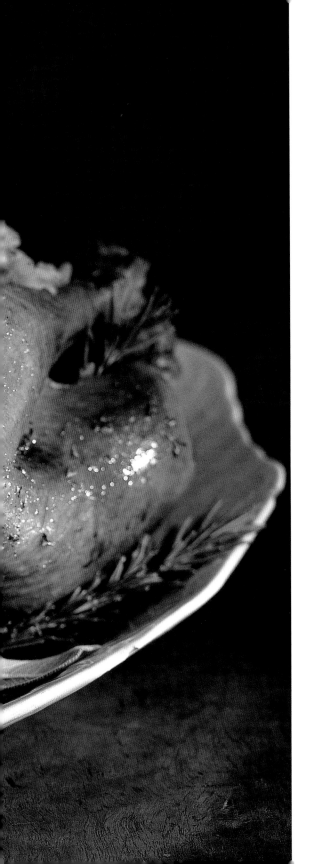

THE MAIN COURSE

When cooking turkey, the centerpiece of every traditional Thanksgiving menu, achieving golden skin, juicy white meat, and well-cooked dark meat all at the same time qualifies as an art. The following recipes come to the aid of the cook, making cooking—and eating—the turkey the best thing that happens all day. (For basic tips on preparing turkey, see pages 110–13.)

CLASSIC ROAST TURKEY
WITH GIBLET GRAVY

BASTING SAVVY
Basting is one of the best ways to ensure that turkey (and other meat and poultry) maintains good flavor and color during roasting. Contrary to popular belief, basting does not add moisture to food, but it does prevent it from losing moisture too quickly as it cooks. Any basting liquids that contain sugar or protein, in the form of butter, corn syrup, honey, preserves, stock or broth, wine, or beer, promote even browning. Basting liquids that contain fat (such as pan drippings) will also add flavor.

Remove the turkey from the refrigerator and let it sit at room temperature for up to 2 hours to take off the chill.

Position a rack in the lower third of the oven and preheat to 325°F (165°C). Rinse the turkey inside and out and pat dry. Trim off and discard excess fat. Fold the wings underneath the back of the turkey to prevent their overbrowning. Lightly salt and pepper the turkey inside and out. Stuff (see Note) and truss the turkey if desired (page 112).

Place the turkey on a rack in a flameproof roasting pan. Spread 2 tablespoons of the butter over the turkey breast. Dampen an 18-inch (45-cm) square of doubled cheesecloth (muslin) and drape it over the turkey breast, leaving the drumsticks uncovered. Place the pan in the oven and roast the turkey for 30 minutes.

Meanwhile, in a small saucepan, combine the chicken broth, the remaining 6 tablespoons (3 oz/90 g) butter, the Port, and the peanut oil. Warm over low heat until the butter has melted.

At the 30-minute mark, using a bulb baster, baste the turkey through the cheesecloth with some of the broth mixture. Continue to roast, basting every 20 minutes, for 1¼ hours. Add the onion and carrots to the roasting pan, stirring to coat them with the drippings. Continue to roast, basting the turkey every 30 minutes with the remaining broth mixture and then with the accumulated pan juices, until the vegetables are well browned and an instant-read thermometer inserted into the thickest part of the turkey thigh away from the bone registers 175°F (80°C), about 1¼ hours longer (for a total roasting time of about 3 hours).

Transfer the turkey to a cutting board and cover it loosely with aluminum foil while you make the gravy.

FOR THE ROAST TURKEY:

1 fresh 12-lb (6-kg) turkey, neck, heart, and gizzard used to make Turkey Stock (page 115), liver reserved

Salt and freshly ground pepper

8 tablespoons (4 oz/125 g) unsalted butter, at room temperature

¾ cup (6 fl oz/180 ml) low-sodium canned chicken broth

½ cup (4 fl oz/125 ml) tawny Port

¼ cup (2 fl oz/60 ml) peanut oil

1 yellow onion, unpeeled, quartered

2 large carrots, unpeeled, coarsely chopped

7 cups (56 fl oz/1.75 l) Turkey Stock (page 115), prepared using tawny Port

¼ cup (1 oz/30 g) cornstarch (cornflour)

Salt and freshly ground pepper

GIBLET GRAVY

To make the gravy, place the roasting pan with the pan juices and vegetables over 2 burners and turn the heat to medium-high. Add all but ¼ cup (2 fl oz/60 ml) of the turkey stock to the roasting pan and bring to a brisk simmer. Stir to deglaze the pan, scraping up the browned bits from the bottom, about 5 minutes.

Pour the contents of the pan through a sieve set over a large bowl, pressing hard on the vegetables with the back of a large spoon to extract all the liquid; discard the solids. Spoon off as much of the fat from the liquid as possible, or pour the liquid into a fat separator and pour off the liquid. Transfer the liquid to a medium saucepan. Place over medium-high heat and simmer briskly for 5 minutes.

Finely chop the heart and gizzard reserved from making the turkey stock and the reserved uncooked liver. Reduce the heat to low and stir the giblets into the gravy. In a small bowl, stir the remaining ¼ cup (2 fl oz/60 ml) stock into the cornstarch to make a slurry. Gradually stir the slurry into the gravy. Cook until the gravy thickens, 3–4 minutes. Season with salt and pepper.

Carve the turkey (page 115) and serve with the gravy.

Note: Stuffing recipes appear on pages 46–53.

Make-Ahead Tip: The stock may be made up to 3 days in advance and refrigerated, or up to 3 months before and frozen. Or, it may be made while the turkey sits before roasting.

MAKES 8–10 SERVINGS

(Photograph appears on following page.)

DEGLAZING FOR GRAVY

Deglazing the roasting pan is in part what makes a gravy rich, brown, and delicious. The cook sets the roasting pan over high heat on the stove top. Pouring a liquid such as stock into the pan, the cook stirs and scrapes to remove all the crusty brown drippings from the bottom of the pan and incorporate them into the sauce. When choosing a pan for roasting, keep this step in mind and choose a sturdy, flameproof pan. You can use disposable aluminum roasting pans, but double up for extra strength.

ROAST TURKEY
WITH CITRUS PAN GRAVY

COMPOUND BUTTERS

Also known as flavored butters, compound butters are blends of unsalted butter with herbs, spices, citrus zest, or other flavorings. Let the butter sit at room temperature for at least 30 minutes to soften, then cream the butter, mashing and beating it with a wooden spoon. When it is soft and fluffy, beat in the flavoring until thoroughly blended. Compound butters are a delicious addition to many foods, from a broiled steak to corn on the cob.

Remove the turkey from the refrigerator and let it sit at room temperature for up to 2 hours to take off the chill.

Position a rack in the lower third of the oven and preheat to 325°F (165°C). Rinse the turkey inside and out and pat dry. Trim off and discard excess fat. Fold the wings underneath the back of the turkey to prevent their overbrowning. Lightly salt and pepper the turkey inside and out. Stuff (see Note) and truss the turkey if desired (page 112).

To make the rosemary-orange butter, mash together the butter, zest, rosemary, and a pinch each of salt and pepper in a bowl.

Working from the tail end of the turkey, gently slide your fingers between the skin and flesh on the breast, legs, and as much of the thighs as you can. Next, slide your fingers between the skin and breast of the turkey from the neck end. Spread about half of the rosemary-orange butter under the skin and over the meat on the turkey breast, legs, and thighs. Spread the remaining butter all over the outside of the skin.

Place the turkey on a rack in a flameproof roasting pan just large enough to hold the turkey. Place the pan in the oven and roast the turkey, rotating the pan's position on the oven rack from front to back several times, for 1¾ hours. Add the onion, orange, and carrots to the pan and continue to roast, stirring the vegetables every 15 minutes, until an instant-read thermometer inserted into the thickest part of the turkey thigh away from the bone registers 175°F (80°C), about 1¼ hours longer (for a total roasting time of about 3 hours).

Transfer the turkey to a cutting board and cover it loosely with aluminum foil while you make the gravy.

1 fresh 12-lb (6-kg) turkey, neck, heart, and gizzard used to make Turkey Stock (page 115)

Salt and freshly ground pepper

FOR THE ROSEMARY-ORANGE BUTTER:

½ cup (4 oz/125 g) unsalted butter, at room temperature

2 tablespoons minced orange zest

4 teaspoons minced fresh rosemary

Salt and freshly ground pepper

1 yellow onion, quartered

1 orange, quartered

3 carrots, unpeeled, coarsely chopped

7 cups (56 fl oz/1.75 l) Turkey Stock (page 115), prepared using dry sherry

¼ cup (2 fl oz/60 ml) fresh orange juice

¼ cup (1 oz/30 g) cornstarch (cornflour)

Salt and freshly ground pepper

CITRUS PAN GRAVY

To make the gravy, place the roasting pan with the pan juices, orange, and vegetables over 2 burners and turn the heat to medium-high. Add the turkey stock to the roasting pan and bring to a brisk simmer. Stir to deglaze the pan, scraping up the browned bits from the bottom, about 5 minutes.

Pour the contents of the pan through a sieve set over a large bowl, pressing hard on the vegetables with the back of a large spoon to extract all the liquid; discard the solids. Spoon off as much of the fat as possible from the liquid, or pour it into a fat separator and pour off the liquid. Transfer the liquid to a medium saucepan. Place over medium-high heat and simmer briskly for 5 minutes.

In a small bowl, stir the orange juice into the cornstarch to make a slurry. Gradually stir the slurry into the simmering gravy. Cook until the gravy thickens, 3–4 minutes. Season the gravy with salt and pepper.

Carve the turkey (page 115) and serve with the gravy.

Note: Stuffing recipes appear on pages 46–53.

Make-Ahead Tips: The stock may be made up to 3 days in advance and refrigerated, or up to 3 months before and frozen. Or, it may be made while the turkey sits before roasting. The rosemary-orange butter can be prepared up to 3 days ahead, covered tightly, and refrigerated. It can also be frozen for up to 1 month. Allow it to sit at room temperature to soften before using.

MAKES 8–10 SERVINGS

(Photograph appears on following page.)

CORNSTARCH

Cornstarch is used in gravy recipes for its thickening power. Just a few spoonfuls can change a thin stock into a thick and shiny sauce. The starch is first blended with a small amount of liquid to make a slurry, a slush that allows smooth blending into the liquid in the pan. After adding the slurry, let the gravy simmer for a few minutes, both to thicken the sauce and to remove the starch's chalky taste. Flour may be used instead, but the amount should be doubled.

BRINED TURKEY BREAST
WITH LEMON-PARSLEY GRAVY

BRINING
Soaking a turkey in a salt-and-sugar solution adds moisture to the meat. This is an especially good technique to use with all-white meat, which can become dry with roasting. Soaking the breasts after brining in fresh water prevents the meat from being overly salty, although it will be somewhat saltier than turkey that has not been brined. Keep this in mind when adding salt to the sauce, to keep the flavors of the dish in balance.

To make the brine, combine the water, salt, and brown sugar in a stockpot. Place over medium heat and cook, stirring, just until the salt and sugar dissolve. Let cool to room temperature.

Rinse the turkey breasts and pat dry. In 1 very large or 2 large glass bowls or other nonaluminum containers, cover the turkey breasts with the brine. Refrigerate, turning the breasts occasionally in the brine, for 24 hours. Drain and discard the brine. Cover the turkey breasts with fresh, cold water and let stand at room temperature, turning once or twice, for 4 hours. Drain and pat dry. Trim excess skin from the turkey breasts.

Position a rack in the lower third of the oven and preheat to 325°F (165°C). Spread 1½ tablespoons of the butter over each turkey breast. Place the breasts on a rack in a flameproof roasting pan. Scatter the onion and carrots in the pan around the turkey. Roast for 30 minutes.

Meanwhile, in a small saucepan, combine the chicken broth, the remaining butter, the white wine, oil, and lemon juice. Warm over low heat until the butter has melted. At the 30-minute mark, baste the breasts with some of the broth mixture.

Continue to roast the turkey, basting every 30 minutes with the remaining broth mixture and then with the accumulated pan juices, stirring the vegetables in the pan occasionally, until the breasts are well browned and an instant-read thermometer inserted into the thickest part of the breast registers 160°F (71°C), about 2 hours total roasting time.

Transfer the breasts to a cutting board and cover them loosely with aluminum foil while you make the gravy.

(Continued on page 39.)

FOR THE BRINE:

6 qt (6 l) water

2 cups (16 oz/500 g) kosher salt

1½ cups (10½ oz/330 g) firmly packed golden brown sugar

2 bone-in fresh whole turkey breasts, about 11 lbs (5.5 kg) total weight

9 tablespoons (4½ oz/140 g) unsalted butter, at room temperature

1 yellow onion, unpeeled, quartered

2 large carrots, unpeeled, coarsely chopped

1¾ cups (14 fl oz/430 ml) low-sodium canned chicken broth

½ cup (4 fl oz/125 ml) dry white wine

¼ cup (2 fl oz/60 ml) peanut or canola oil

1 tablespoon fresh lemon juice

7 cups (56 fl oz/1.75 l) Turkey Stock (page 115)

¼ cup (1 oz/30 g) corn-starch (cornflour)

⅓ cup (½ oz/15 g) minced fresh flat-leaf (Italian) parsley

1 tablespoon fresh lemon juice

1 tablespoon minced lemon zest

Salt and freshly ground pepper

LEMON-PARSLEY GRAVY

(Continued from page 36.)

To make the gravy, place the roasting pan with the vegetables across 2 burners and turn the heat to medium-high. Add all but ¼ cup (2 fl oz/60 ml) of the turkey stock to the pan and bring to a brisk simmer. Stir to deglaze the pan, scraping up the browned bits from the bottom, about 5 minutes.

Pour the contents of the pan through a sieve set over a large bowl, pressing hard on the vegetables with the back of a large spoon to extract all the liquid; discard the solids. Spoon off as much of the fat as possible from the liquid, or pour the liquid into a fat separator and pour off the liquid. Transfer the liquid to a wide saucepan. Place over medium-high heat and simmer briskly until reduced by one-fourth, about 10 minutes.

In a small bowl, stir the remaining ¼ cup (2 fl oz/60 ml) stock into the cornstarch to make a slurry. Gradually stir the slurry into the simmering gravy. Stir in the parsley, lemon juice, and the lemon zest. Cook until the gravy clears and thickens, about 1 minute. Season with salt and pepper.

Slice the turkey breast against the grain, on a slight diagonal, and serve with the gravy.

Make-Ahead Tips: The turkey must be put into the brine 28 hours before cooking. The stock may be made up to 3 days in advance and refrigerated, or up to 3 months before and frozen. Or, it may be made while the breasts soak in fresh water before roasting.

MAKES 8-10 SERVINGS

PARSLEY VARIETIES

Two types of parsley are commonly available: curly-leaf parsley and flat-leaf, or Italian, parlsey. In past years, the curly variety was the one most often used to garnish plates in the United States. Many cooks are now coming around to using flat-leaf parsley for its more pronounced flavor. Parsley has a clean, fresh taste that pairs well with the lemon in this gravy.

HICKORY-SMOKED TURKEY
WITH HORSERADISH-APPLE SAUCE

HOME-SMOKING

Expect the meat of this turkey to have a pinkish color, as is typical for home-smoked birds. Although the skin will have a shiny, rich mahogany color, it will be too leathery and smoky for most diners' tastes and may simply be removed and discarded before carving. Serve the turkey hot, warm, or at room temperature. Cooked mainly on the grill, this turkey leaves the oven free most of the time for pies, dressing, or other dishes—a boon on this day of oven gridlock.

Let the turkey sit at room temperature for up to 2 hours to take off the chill. Rinse the bird inside and out and pat dry. Trim off and discard excess fat. Fold the wings underneath the back. Lightly salt and pepper the turkey inside and out.

Light a fire in a large charcoal grill with a cover. When the coals are white, bank them on two sides of the fuel bed to create a cool zone in the center. Drain the hickory wood and place 3 chunks atop each bank of coals. Put the grill rack in place and cover the grill. Preheat until a built-in grill thermometer or oven thermometer placed inside the grill registers 250°F (120°C). Put the turkey in a roasting pan and place on the grill rack over the cool zone. Cover the grill and smoke the turkey, rotating the pan occasionally to expose the bird to the smoke evenly, for 3 hours. During this time, uncover the grill no more than is necessary (to avoid heat loss) and maintain its temperature at about 250°F (120°C), regulating the level by adjusting the upper and lower vents. Light more charcoal briquettes in a chimney starter and add them to the grill as needed to maintain the heat.

To make the sauce, in a bowl, stir together all the ingredients, including pepper to taste. Cover and refrigerate until using.

Near the end of the 3-hour period, preheat an oven to 325°F (165°C). Transfer the turkey from the grill to the oven without allowing it to cool and bake until an instant-read thermometer inserted into the thickest part of the thigh away from the bone registers 175°F (80°C), 30–40 minutes. Do not overcook. Remove the turkey from the oven and let rest, loosely covered with foil, for at least 10 minutes before carving (page 115). Serve with the horseradish sauce.

MAKES 8-10 SERVINGS

1 fresh 12-lb (6-kg) turkey

Salt and freshly ground pepper

Six 3-inch (7.5-cm) chunks hickory wood, soaked in water to cover for 24 hours

FOR THE SAUCE:

2 jars (8 oz/250 g each) prepared cream-style horseradish

½ cup (4 oz/125 g) sour cream

½ cup (4 fl oz/125 ml) mayonnaise

1 crisp red-skinned apple such as Delicious, cored and coarsely grated

1 tablespoon thinly sliced fresh chives

1 teaspoon sugar

Freshly ground pepper

BAKED HAM
WITH HONEY-BRANDY GLAZE

1 fully cooked bone-in 18-lb (9-kg) smoked ham

About 36 whole cloves (optional)

3 cups (24 fl oz/750 ml) water

1 cup (8 fl oz/250 ml) brandy

1 cup (8 fl oz/250 ml) unfiltered apple cider

¾ cup (9 oz/280 g) honey

Position a rack in the lower third of the oven and preheat to 325°F (165°C). Slice away the rind (if any) and most of the fat from the upper surface of the ham, leaving a layer of fat about ¼ inch (6 mm) thick. With a sharp knife, shallowly score the upper surface of the ham into a diamond pattern. If desired, insert a clove into the center of each diamond.

Place the ham on a rack in a shallow roasting pan just large enough to hold it comfortably. Add the water to the pan and place it in the oven. Bake for 2¼ hours.

Meanwhile, in a measuring pitcher, stir together the brandy, cider, and honey. At the 2¼-hour mark, pour off the water from the roasting pan. Baste the ham with about one-third of the brandy mixture and bake for 12 minutes. Continue to bake, basting the ham with the brandy mixture at 12-minute intervals, first from the measuring pitcher and then from the roasting pan, until the ham is glazed and shiny, for another 35 minutes or so (for a total baking time of about 3 hours).

Let the ham rest on a cutting board for 15 minutes. For easier carving, remove most of the cloves (if used), leaving a few for decoration. Serve hot or warm.

Make-Ahead Tip: Since the ham is as good warm as it is hot (and since it stays hot for at least 1 hour after baking), don't hesitate to let it rest, uncarved, while you use the oven for side dishes.

MAKES 10 SERVINGS (PLUS AMPLE LEFTOVERS)

HAM

A baked ham can be a festive alternative to the traditional Thanksgiving turkey. Although the ham used in this recipe is already fully cooked, baking it for 10 minutes per pound (500 g) not only improves the texture and flavor, making it tender and succulent, but also allows you to coat it with a shiny and flavorful glaze. Look for a cooked, smoked ham, sometimes labeled "water added," not a country ham or dry-aged ham such as Smithfield. You may need to order a whole ham in advance from the butcher.

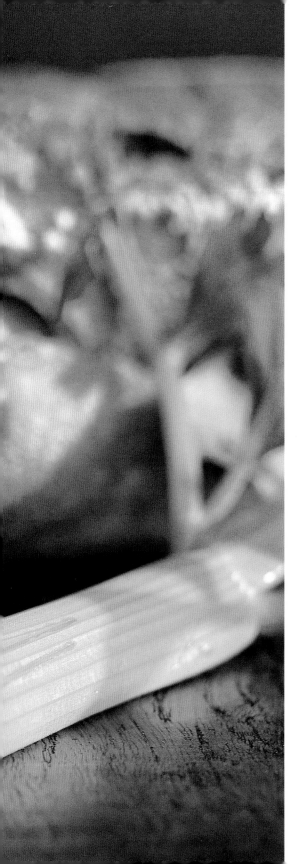

DRESSINGS, STUFFINGS, AND BREADS

Moist and savory, bread-based dressings (or stuffings) are many people's favorite element of the Thanksgiving dinner. And the rolls, biscuits, and corn bread that have all but disappeared from the daily menu in modern times return for the holiday feast.

BREAD DRESSING WITH CELERY

DRESSING OR STUFFING?

Some folks define dressing as stuffing that is cooked outside of the bird in a baking dish, although in many regions the two terms are interchangeable. The advantage to baking the dressing in a separate container is that it allows for faster roasting and more accurate timing of the turkey. When dressing is baked in a well-buttered dish, it acquires lots of crisp brown crust that contrasts deliciously with the rich, moist interior. For complete information about stuffing a bird, see page 112.

In a large frying pan over medium heat, melt the ¾ cup butter. Add the onion, celery, poultry seasoning, and thyme. Cover and cook, stirring once or twice, until tender, about 15 minutes. Remove from the heat and let cool to room temperature.

Using a serrated knife, trim the crusts from the bread and cut the slices into ½-inch (12-mm) cubes. In a very large bowl, combine the bread and the onion mixture.

In another bowl, whisk the eggs until blended. Whisk in the stock. Stir the stock mixture into the bread mixture. Add the parsley, 2 teaspoons salt, and 1½ teaspoons pepper. Stir well, breaking down the bread cubes to form a soft mass.

To bake the dressing alongside a turkey in a 325°F (165°C) oven, generously grease a 4-qt (4-l) baking dish. Spoon the dressing into the prepared dish and cover tightly with aluminum foil. Bake for 45 minutes. Uncover and continue to bake until the dressing is steaming hot, lightly browned on top, and well browned on the sides and bottom but still moist, 30–35 minutes longer. Serve hot.

To bake the dressing in a turkey, loosely stuff the turkey's cavities with dressing and truss the larger opening (page 112); increase the roasting time of the turkey by 35–45 minutes. Generously butter a baking dish large enough to hold the remaining dressing and spoon in the dressing. Cover tightly with aluminum foil and bake alongside the turkey for 45 minutes. Uncover and bake until the dressing is steaming hot, lightly browned on top, and well browned on the sides and bottom but still moist, another 30–35 minutes, depending on the size of the baking dish. Serve hot.

MAKES 8–10 SERVINGS

¾ cup (6 oz/185 g) unsalted butter, plus extra for greasing

4 cups (1¼ lb/625 g) finely chopped yellow onion

2 cups (12 oz/375 g) finely chopped celery, including some leafy tops

5 teaspoons poultry seasoning

2 teaspoons dried thyme

3 lb (1.5 kg) firm white sandwich bread slices, 2 or 3 days old

5 eggs

6 cups (48 fl oz/1.5 l) chicken stock or low-sodium canned chicken broth

½ cup (⅔ oz/20 g) minced fresh flat-leaf (Italian) parsley

Salt and freshly ground pepper

WILD RICE AND CHESTNUT DRESSING

6 cups (48 fl oz/1.5 l) water

1½ cups (10 oz/315 g) jumbo-grade wild rice, rinsed until water runs clear

Salt and freshly ground pepper

½ cup (4 oz/125 g) unsalted butter, plus extra for greasing

4 cups (1¼ lb/625 g) finely chopped yellow onion

2 cups (12 oz/375 g) finely chopped fennel

1 tablespoon poultry seasoning

1 teaspoon dried thyme

½ teaspoon fennel seeds

1½ lb (750 g) firm whole-wheat (wholemeal) sand-wich bread, 2 or 3 days old

1½ lb (750 g) fresh chest-nuts, cooked and peeled (page 71), or 3 cups (15 oz/470 g) purchased steamed chestnuts

5 eggs

4 cups (32 fl oz/1 l) chicken stock or low-sodium canned chicken broth

¼ cup (⅓ oz/10 g) finely chopped fresh flat-leaf (Italian) parsley

In a heavy pot over high heat, bring the water to a boil. Add the wild rice and 2 teaspoons salt. Cover partially, reduce the heat to low, and cook, stirring occasionally, until the rice is done to your liking, about 45 minutes for a fairly firm texture. Drain and let cool.

In a large frying pan over medium heat, melt the ½ cup butter. Add the onion, fennel, poultry seasoning, thyme, and fennel seeds. Cover and cook, stirring once or twice, until the vegetables are tender, about 15 minutes. Remove from the heat and let cool.

Using a serrated knife, trim the crusts from the bread and cut the slices into ½-inch (12-mm) cubes. In a very large bowl, combine the bread, rice, chestnuts, and the onion mixture. In another bowl, whisk the eggs until blended. Whisk the stock into the eggs and stir the egg mixture into the bowl with the bread mixture. Stir in the parsley, 2 teaspoons salt, and 1½ teaspoons pepper.

To bake the dressing alongside a turkey in a 325°F (165°C) oven, generously grease a 4-qt (4-l) baking dish. Spoon the bread mixture into the prepared dish and cover tightly with foil. Bake for 40 minutes. Uncover and continue to bake until the dressing is steaming hot, lightly browned on top, and well browned on the sides, another 30–40 minutes. Serve hot.

To bake the dressing in a turkey, loosely stuff the turkey's cavities with the mixture and truss the larger opening (page 112); increase the roasting time of the turkey by 35–45 minutes. Generously butter a baking dish large enough to hold the remaining dressing and spoon in the dressing. Cover tightly with foil and bake alongside the turkey for 30 minutes. Uncover and bake until the dressing is steaming hot, lightly browned on top, and well browned on the sides and bottom but still moist, another 25–35 minutes. Serve hot.

MAKES 10 SERVINGS

WILD RICE

Wild rice is not a rice at all, but the seed of an aquatic grass. Although much of it is now cultivated and harvested by machine, it can still be found wild along the shore-lines of lakes and rivers in the American Midwest, particularly in Minnesota. There, it is still gathered by hand by Native Americans working from canoes. Jumbo-grade grains are the longest and most desirable for this stuffing. Doneness is a matter of per-sonal taste, with some cooks preferring the rice still slightly crunchy, others liking it cooked until it is tender and the ends of the grains have split.

SOURDOUGH DRESSING
WITH SAUSAGE AND PRUNES

In a frying pan over medium heat, cook the sausage, stirring it occasionally without breaking up too much, until just cooked through and lightly browned, about 10 minutes. Transfer the sausage to paper towels to drain. Discard the drippings. Return the pan to medium heat and heat the ½ cup butter until it foams. Stir in the onion and poultry seasoning, cover, and cook, stirring occasionally, until the onion is tender, 12–15 minutes. Let cool.

In a large bowl, combine the bread, sausage, and onion mixture. In another bowl, lightly beat the eggs. Whisk the stock into the eggs and stir the stock mixture into the bread mixture. Add the prunes, 2 teaspoons salt, and 1 teaspoon pepper and mix well.

To bake the dressing alongside a turkey in a 325°F (165°C) oven, generously grease a deep 4-qt (4-l) baking dish. Spoon the mixture into the prepared dish and cover tightly with aluminum foil. Bake for 45 minutes. Uncover and continue to bake until the dressing is lightly browned on top and well browned on the sides and bottom but still moist, about another 25 minutes. Remove from the oven and let stand on a wire rack for 5 minutes before serving. Serve hot.

To bake the dressing in a turkey, loosely stuff the turkey with dressing and truss the larger opening (page 112); increase the roasting time of the turkey by 35–45 minutes. Generously butter a baking dish and spoon in the remaining dressing. Cover tightly with aluminum foil and bake alongside the turkey for 45 minutes. Uncover and bake until the dressing is steaming hot, lightly browned on top, and well browned on the sides and bottom but still moist, about another 25 minutes, depending on the size of the baking dish. Serve hot.

MAKES 8–10 SERVINGS

PRUNES

Prunes are dried plums—in particular, the small purple plums called prune plums. Prunes appear in both sweet and savory dishes and are often paired with pork, as in this recipe. Dried apricots can replace some or all of the prunes in the dressing, if desired.

1 lb (500 g) bulk breakfast sausage with sage, coarsely crumbled

½ cup (4 oz/125 g) unsalted butter, plus extra for greasing

4 cups (1¼ lb/625 g) finely chopped yellow onion

2 tablespoons poultry seasoning

2½ lb (1.25 kg) sourdough bread slices, 2 or 3 days old, crusts trimmed and bread cut into ½-inch (12-mm) cubes

5 eggs

5 cups (40 fl oz/1.25 l) chicken stock or low-sodium canned chicken broth

2 cups (12 oz/375 g) quartered pitted prunes

Salt and freshly ground pepper

CORN BREAD DRESSING
WITH OYSTERS AND HAM

6 tablespoons (3 oz/90 g) unsalted butter, plus extra for greasing

¼ lb (125 g) firm, smoky baked ham, diced

2 cups (10 oz/315 g) finely chopped yellow onion

2 red bell peppers (capsicums), seeded and chopped

1 bunch green (spring) onions, including tender green parts, thinly sliced

1¼ teaspoons dried thyme

5 cups (10 oz/315 g) crumbled day-old Buttermilk Corn Bread (page 61)

4 cups (8 oz/250 g) torn-up slightly dry firm white bread

18 oysters, freshly shucked, with liquor reserved *(far right)*

About 2 cups (16 fl oz/ 500 ml) chicken stock or low-sodium canned chicken broth

3 eggs, well beaten

Salt and freshly ground pepper

In a large frying pan over medium heat, melt the 6 tablespoons butter. Add the ham and sauté until lightly browned, 8–10 minutes. Add the yellow onion, bell peppers, green onions, and thyme. Cover and cook, stirring once or twice, until the vegetables are tender, about 10 minutes. Remove from the heat and let cool.

In a large bowl, toss together the corn bread, white bread, and ham mixture with any juices from the pan.

Line a fine-mesh sieve with cheesecloth (muslin), place over a measuring pitcher, and strain the oyster liquor through it. Add enough stock to the oyster liquor to equal 2 cups (16 fl oz/500 ml). Combine this liquid and the eggs and pour over the bread mixture. Add 1 teaspoon salt and ¾ teaspoon pepper and stir again.

To bake the dressing alongside a turkey in a 325°F (165°C) oven, position a rack in the upper third of the oven. Generously grease a 9-by-13-inch (23-by-33-cm) baking dish. Spoon half of the dressing into the prepared dish. Space the oysters evenly over the dressing without letting them touch the sides of the dish. Spoon the remaining dressing over the oysters, spreading it to the edges of the dish. Bake until the dressing is steaming and the top is lightly browned, about 1 hour. Let stand for 5 minutes, then serve hot.

To bake the dressing in a turkey, mix the oysters into the bread mixture. Loosely stuff the turkey with dressing and truss the larger opening (page 112); increase the roasting time of the turkey by 35–45 minutes. Generously butter a baking dish and spoon in the remaining dressing. Bake uncovered until the dressing is steaming and the top is lightly browned, about 1 hour, depending on the size of the baking dish. Serve hot.

MAKES 8–10 SERVINGS

SHUCKING OYSTERS
Protect your nondominant hand with a kitchen towel. Hold the oyster in this hand, flat side up, with the narrow hinge end toward you. Insert an oyster knife between the shell halves, just beside the hinge. Gently twist the knife and the halves will separate. Pour out and reserve the oyster liquor. Run the knife along the inside top shell to cut the muscle, then slip the knife between the oyster and the bottom shell to release it. If fresh oysters are not available, look for refrigerated jarred oysters.

POPOVERS

Butter a standard-sized, 12-cup popover pan or muffin pan. In a bowl, combine the eggs and salt. Using a whisk, beat lightly. Stir in the milk and butter, then beat in the flour just until blended. Do not overbeat.

Fill each popover cup about half full and place in a cold oven *(left)*. Set the oven temperature to 425°F (220°C) and bake for 20 minutes. Reduce the heat to 375°F (190°C) and continue to bake until the popovers are golden, 10–15 minutes longer. They should be crisp on the outside.

Quickly pierce each popover with a thin metal skewer or the tip of a small knife to release the steam. Leave in the oven for a couple of minutes for further crisping, then remove and serve at once.

MAKES 12 POPOVERS

2 eggs

¼ teaspoon salt

1 cup (8 fl oz/250 ml) milk

2 tablespoons unsalted butter, melted

1 cup (5 oz/155 g) all-purpose (plain) flour

POPOVER SAVVY

Like many other quick breads, popovers are best when baked directly after mixing. According to famed cookbook author Marion Cunningham, the best way to bake popovers is to start them in a cold oven. If this doesn't work in your Thanksgiving Day cooking schedule, they may be baked in a preheated oven, but check them after 25 minutes to be sure they are not done early.

POPPY-SEED CLOVERLEAF ROLLS

1 cup (8 fl oz/250 ml) milk

2 tablespoons unsalted butter, plus extra for greasing

1 tablespoon sugar

1 package (2½ teaspoons) active dry yeast

¾ teaspoon salt

2¾ cups (14 oz/440 g) unbleached all-purpose (plain) flour, plus extra as needed

1 teaspoon corn oil

1 egg, well beaten

1¼ teaspoons poppy seeds

In a small saucepan, combine the milk, the 2 tablespoons butter, and the sugar. Warm over low heat just until the butter melts. Transfer to a bowl and let cool to 105°–115°F (40°–46°C). Sprinkle the yeast over the milk mixture. Whisk in the yeast and let stand until foamy, about 5 minutes. Whisk again and then stir in the salt and the flour, ½ cup (2½ oz/75 g) at a time, until a soft, sticky dough forms.

Turn the dough out onto a well-floured surface and knead it, incorporating 1 tablespoonful more of the flour at a time as necessary, until it is smooth, elastic, and no longer sticky, about 5 minutes. Coat a bowl with the oil, add the dough, turn to coat it with the oil, and cover with plastic wrap or a damp kitchen towel. Let rise in a warm place until doubled, about 1½ hours.

Generously grease the cups of a 12-cup muffin pan. Turn the dough out onto a floured surface and flatten it into a round. Divide the round into 12 equal portions. Divide each portion into thirds. Shape the pieces into balls and place 3 balls in each cup of the prepared pan. Cover with a kitchen towel and let rise in a warm place until doubled, about 1 hour.

Preheat the oven to 375°F (190°C). Brush the tops of the rolls with the egg. Sprinkle the poppy seeds over the rolls, dividing them evenly. Bake until the rolls are puffed and golden and the bottoms and sides are crisp, about 15 minutes. Remove from the pan immediately. Serve hot or warm.

Make-Ahead Tip: The rolls can be baked 1 day in advance. Let cool completely, then wrap them airtight and store at room temperature. Wrap tightly in aluminum foil and rewarm in a 350°F (180°C) oven for 15 minutes.

MAKES 12 ROLLS

PROOFING YEAST

Yeast is proofed, or tested, by letting the granules stand in warm water for 5 minutes, until they turn foamy. Yeast was not always as reliable as it is now, and proofing was an essential step that saved the cook from rolls or loaves that failed to rise. Now, yeast is more consistent, but because it gradually weakens the longer it sits on a pantry shelf, it's a good idea to be sure that yeast is alive and active, and to give it a head start before it is incorporated into the flour.

SWEET POTATO BISCUITS

Preheat the oven to 400°F (200°C). Prick the sweet potato several times with a fork. Place it directly on the oven rack and bake until very tender, about 1¼ hours. Let cool completely.

Position a rack in the upper third of the oven and raise the oven temperature to 450°F (230°C). Peel the sweet potato and force it through the medium disk of a food mill or a large-mesh sieve into a bowl. Add the buttermilk and whisk until smooth.

In a large bowl, sift together the all-purpose flour, cake flour, baking powder, sugar, and salt. Add the shortening and butter and, using a pastry cutter, cut them into the dry ingredients until the pieces of fat resemble corn kernels. Add the buttermilk mixture and stir until a soft, crumbly dough forms. Turn the dough out onto a well-floured surface and knead 8–10 times, until it just holds together.

Roll and pat the dough out into a rectangle 6 by 12 inches (15 by 30 cm) in area. Using a knife or cookie cutter, cut the dough into 12 rectangular biscuits. Transfer the biscuits to an ungreased insulated baking sheet or doubled regular baking sheet. Bake until the biscuits have risen and their edges and bottoms are lightly browned, 12–14 minutes.

Meanwhile, make the honey butter. In a small bowl, cream together the butter and honey until light and fluffy. Serve the biscuits hot, accompanied with the honey butter.

Make-Ahead Tip: The sweet potato can be baked 1 day ahead and kept at room temperature. The dry and wet mixtures can be prepared several hours in advance, but do not combine them until you are ready to bake. The honey butter can be prepared several days ahead and refrigerated.

MAKES 12 BISCUITS

1 sweet potato (about 8 oz/250 g)

1¼ cups (10 fl oz/310 ml) buttermilk

2½ cups (12½ oz/390 g) unbleached all-purpose (plain) flour

1 cup (4 oz/125 g) cake (soft-wheat) flour

5 teaspoons baking powder

4 teaspoons sugar

¾ teaspoon salt

⅔ cup (6 oz/185 g) cold solid vegetable shortening, cut into small pieces

¼ cup (2 oz/60 g) cold unsalted butter, cut into small pieces

FOR THE HONEY BUTTER:

¾ cup (6 oz/185 g) unsalted butter, at room temperature

⅓ cup (4 oz/125 g) honey

BISCUIT SAVVY

A few tips will result in great biscuits. Keeping the fats cold gives the biscuits flakiness. Handling the dough as little as possible keeps the biscuits tender. Some recipes call for gathering and rerolling scraps, which can lead to tough biscuits; cutting rectangular biscuits is a clever way to avoid this, as rectangles leave no scraps. Cutting the biscuits with a straight-down motion ensures an even shape, and baking them at high heat results in biscuits that rise high and brown handsomely.

BUTTERMILK CORN BREAD

½ cup (4 oz/125 g) unsalted butter, melted and cooled slightly, plus extra for greasing

2 cups (10 oz/315 g) yellow cornmeal, preferably stone ground

1 cup (5 oz/155 g) unbleached all-purpose (plain) flour

⅓ cup (3 oz/90 g) sugar

4 teaspoons baking powder

1 teaspoon salt

1½ cups (12 fl oz/375 ml) buttermilk, at room temperature

2 eggs, at room temperature, well beaten

Preheat the oven to 400°F (200°C). Grease a 9-by-13-inch (23-by-33-cm) metal baking pan.

In a large bowl, thoroughly stir together the cornmeal, flour, sugar, baking powder, and salt. In another bowl, mix together the buttermilk, eggs, and melted butter until just combined. Stir the wet ingredients into the dry ingredients just until combined. Spread the batter in the prepared pan.

Bake until the edges of the corn bread are just beginning to pull away from the sides of the pan and a knife inserted at the center comes out clean, 18–20 minutes. Let stand in the pan for at least 5 minutes, then, placing a baking sheet over the pan, carefully invert the pan and sheet and let the corn bread fall onto the sheet. Cut into squares and serve hot or warm.

Make-Ahead Tip: This corn bread can be used as the main ingredient in Corn Bread Dressing with Oysters and Ham, page 53.

MAKES 8–10 SERVINGS

STONE-GROUND CORNMEAL

In a bread this simple, the quality of the ingredients shows. Stone-ground cornmeal is more perishable, since it contains the germ of the corn, but its coarser texture and more intense corn flavor make it a good choice here. Look for it in well-stocked supermarkets and in natural-foods stores.

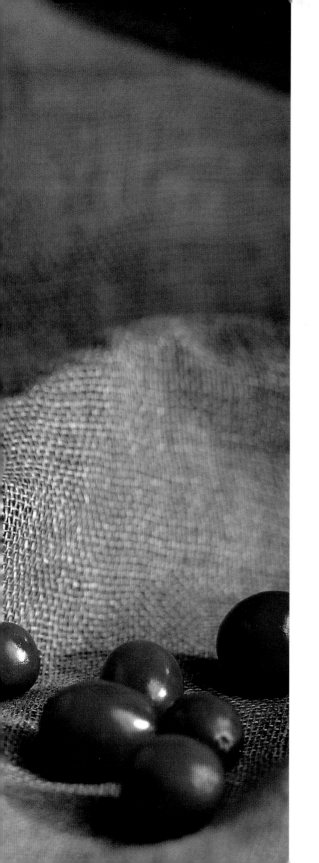

VEGETABLES
AND RELISHES

Vegetable dishes and relishes play an important role in balancing the Thanksgiving menu, providing bright color and a pleasant crunch. Some of the following dishes are spicy, others light—a bit of each is nice, and there should be a generous array.

MAPLE-GLAZED CARROTS

In a large saucepan over medium heat, combine the carrots, stock, maple syrup, and butter. Bring to a brisk simmer and cook, uncovered, until the carrots are tender, about 30 minutes.

Using a slotted spoon, transfer the carrots to a dish. Raise the heat to high and cook the liquid in the pan until it has reduced to about 1¼ cups (10 fl oz/310 ml) and is syrupy, 30–40 minutes longer.

Return the carrots to the pan. Add the vinegar and ½ teaspoon pepper. Taste and adjust the seasoning with salt and pepper (the dish may not need additional salt). Serve hot.

Make-Ahead Tip: This dish can be prepared through the step of reducing the sauce several hours in advance. Return the carrots to the reduced sauce, remove the pan from the heat, and let cool to room temperature. Just before serving, stir in the vinegar and pepper and reheat the carrots just until warmed through.

MAKES 8–10 SERVINGS

3 lb (1.5 kg) carrots, peeled and cut on the diagonal into 1-inch (2.5-cm) pieces

5 cups (40 fl oz/1.25 l) chicken stock or low-sodium canned chicken broth

¾ cup (6 fl oz/180 ml) pure maple syrup

5 tablespoons (2½ oz/75 g) unsalted butter

1½ tablespoons cider vinegar

Salt and freshly ground pepper

PURE MAPLE SYRUP

Pure maple syrup is made from the boiled sap of the sugar maple tree and has a flavor reminiscent of vanilla and caramel. In early spring, throughout Canada and the northern United States, taps for collecting sap appear on the trunks of maple trees. The clear, fresh sap is boiled down until it is reduced to a rich, aromatic, amber syrup.

Maple syrup is graded according to its quality and color. In general, the lighter the color, the milder-tasting the syrup and the higher the grade. Use lighter syrups on pancakes and darker ones for cooking.

GREEN BEANS WITH PECANS

Salt and freshly ground pepper

2 lb (1 kg) green beans, trimmed and halved on the diagonal

5 tablespoons (2½ oz/75 g) unsalted butter

1 cup (4 oz/125 g) chopped pecans

Bring a large pot three-fourths full of water to a boil. Salt the water, add the beans, and cook until crisp-tender, 4 or 5 minutes.

Drain, transfer immediately to a bowl of ice water, and let cool for 1 minute. Drain again and pat dry.

In a large frying pan over medium heat, melt the butter. Add the pecans and cook, stirring often, until the nuts are lightly browned and fragrant, about 5 minutes. Add the beans and toss to coat with the butter. Add ¾ teaspoon salt and ½ teaspoon pepper, cover partially, and cook, tossing and stirring occasionally, until the beans are heated through, another 5 or 6 minutes.

Taste and adjust the seasoning with salt and pepper. Serve hot.

MAKES 8–10 SERVINGS

GREEN BEANS

Sometimes called string beans, green beans did indeed once have tough strings that needed to be pulled off before cooking. Nowadays, the beans are bred so that the strings are nonexistent. The beans need only to have their ends trimmed—or, if desired, only the stem ends trimmed—before being cooked whole or cut into pieces, as called for in a recipe.

BRUSSELS SPROUTS
IN WHITE CHEDDAR SAUCE

Cut a shallow X in the stem end of each Brussels sprout. Bring a large saucepan three-fourths full of water to a boil. Salt the water, add the Brussels sprouts, and cook until just tender, 6–8 minutes. Drain and transfer to a bowl of ice water. When cool, drain again and thoroughly pat dry.

In a small, heavy saucepan over low heat, melt 2 tablespoons of the butter. Whisk in the flour and cook, stirring constantly, for 3 minutes. Do not let the flour brown. Remove the pan from the heat and gradually whisk in the milk. Set the pan over medium heat. Whisk in ¼ teaspoon salt, ¼ teaspoon pepper, and the nutmeg. Bring to a simmer, whisking constantly. Reduce the heat to low, cover partially, and cook, whisking occasionally, until thick and smooth, about 15 minutes. Remove from the heat, add the cheese, and whisk until the cheese is melted.

In a large frying pan over medium heat, melt the remaining 4 tablespoons (2 oz/60 g) butter. Add the Brussels sprouts, cover, and cook, rolling them around, until they are heated through and just beginning to brown, 6–8 minutes. Remove the pan from the heat, let cool for 1 minute, and then stir the cheese sauce into the Brussels sprouts. Set the pan over low heat and cook, stirring often, until heated through, about 2 minutes. Taste and adjust the seasoning. Serve hot.

Make-Ahead Tips: The Brussels sprouts can be prepared through the step of placing them in ice water 1 day in advance. Drain, pat dry, cover, and refrigerate. The cheese sauce can be prepared several hours in advance. Let cool, then cover with plastic wrap, pressing it directly onto the surface of the sauce to prevent a skin from forming. Hold at room temperature until ready to complete the recipe.

MAKES 8–10 SERVINGS

NUTMEG

The seed of a tropical evergreen tree, nutmeg is grown in Indonesia, the Philippines, and on the Caribbean island of Grenada. When first removed from the fruit, the nutmeg is enclosed in a lacy red cage that, when lifted away and ground, is known as the spice mace. Nutmeg tastes "warm" and is often used in holiday baking. In very small amounts, such as in the sauce for the Brussels sprouts, it acts as a subtle flavor booster. Nutmeg should always be grated fresh just before using.

3 lb (1.5 kg) Brussels sprouts, stems trimmed and outer brown leaves removed

Salt and freshly ground pepper

6 tablespoons (3 oz/90 g) unsalted butter

2 tablespoons all-purpose (plain) flour

2 cups (16 fl oz/500 ml) milk

Pinch of freshly grated nutmeg

1½ cups (6 oz/185 g) shredded sharp white Cheddar cheese

BRAISED CHESTNUTS WITH MADEIRA CREAM SAUCE

½ cup (4 oz/125 g) unsalted butter

1½ lb (750 g) shiitake mushrooms, brushed clean, stems removed, and caps quartered

Salt and freshly ground pepper

1 lb (500 g) carrots, peeled and cut on the diagonal into 1-inch (2.5-cm) pieces

⅓ cup (2 oz/60 g) minced shallot

1¼ cups (10 fl oz/310 ml) chicken stock or low-sodium canned chicken broth

¾ cup (6 fl oz/180 ml) plus 2 tablespoons medium-dry Madeira wine

4 teaspoons cornstarch (cornflour)

¼ cup (2 fl oz/60 ml) heavy (double) cream

1½ lb (750 g) fresh chest-nuts, roasted and peeled *(far right)*, or 3 cups (15 oz/470 g) purchased steamed chestnuts

In a large frying pan over medium-high heat, melt half the butter. Add the mushrooms and ½ teaspoon salt, cover, and cook, stirring once or twice, until the mushrooms are tender and lightly browned, about 7 minutes. Transfer to a bowl and set aside.

Return the frying pan to medium heat and add the remaining butter. When it has melted, add the carrots, cover, and cook, stirring once or twice and not allowing the butter to brown, for 15 minutes. Add the shallot, cover, and cook for 5 minutes. Add the stock, the ¾ cup Madeira, and the mushrooms. Bring to a simmer and cook uncovered, stirring once or twice, until the carrots are almost tender, about 12 minutes.

In a small bowl, stir the 2 tablespoons Madeira into the cornstarch to make a slurry. Add the slurry and the cream to the frying pan. Scatter the chestnuts over the mushrooms and carrots. Bring to a simmer, cover, and cook, stirring occasionally, until the sauce has thickened, about 5 minutes. Season the sauce generously with pepper. Taste and adjust the seasoning with salt.

Fold the chestnuts into the sauce, breaking them up as little as possible. Transfer to a warmed bowl and serve immediately.

MAKES 8–10 SERVINGS

ROASTED AND PEELED CHESTNUTS

To prepare fresh chestnuts, with a sharp knife, score a shallow X across the flat side of each chestnut, cutting all the way through to the meat. Soak in cold water to cover for 15 minutes, drain, and spread out on a baking sheet in a single layer. Roast in a preheated 400°F (200°C) oven, stirring once or twice, until the peels have curled open along the cut marks and the nuts give slightly when pressed, 10–12 minutes. Cool slightly, then remove the outer and inner peels.

BROCCOLI WITH A CRUNCHY CRUMB TOPPING

Cut off the broccoli stems and reserve for another use. Separate the heads into florets.

Bring a large pot three-fourths full of water to a boil. Salt the water and add the broccoli. Cook, stirring once or twice, until just tender, 4–6 minutes. Drain and transfer to a bowl of ice water. When cool, drain again and pat dry.

In a large frying pan over medium-high heat, melt the ½ cup butter. Add the orange zest and garlic and cook, stirring once or twice, until the butter begins to brown, about 3 minutes. Add the bread crumbs and stir to moisten. Cook, stirring occasionally, until crisp and golden brown, about 5 minutes. Stir in ¼ teaspoon salt and a generous grinding of pepper. Remove from the heat and keep warm.

Meanwhile, in a large frying pan, melt the remaining 6 tablespoons butter. Add the broccoli, cover the pan, and cook, tossing and stirring occasionally, until heated through and glazed with butter, 5 minutes. Season with ¼ teaspoon salt and a generous grinding of pepper and toss again.

Spoon the broccoli into a warmed wide serving bowl. Spoon the bread crumbs evenly over the broccoli and serve immediately.

Make-Ahead Tip: The broccoli can be prepared through the step of placing it in ice water up to 1 day ahead. Drain, pat dry, cover, and refrigerate. Return to room temperature before proceeding. The bread crumbs can be prepared several hours in advance and then reheated just before serving.

MAKES 8–10 SERVINGS

ZESTING CITRUS

If possible, choose organic fruit for zesting, and be sure to scrub the fruit well to remove any residue or wax. Cut off only the thin, colored part of the rind, taking care not to include the bitter white pith. You can use a zester, a tool designed to remove the zest in long, narrow strips, which can then be left whole or chopped. A paring knife or vegetable peeler can also be used, but both often produce short, wide pieces that need further slicing. Zest can be removed with the fine rasps of a handheld grater as well.

3 large bunches broccoli (about 10 stalks)

Salt and freshly ground pepper

½ cup (4 oz/125 g) plus 6 tablespoons (3 oz/90 g) unsalted butter

2 tablespoons finely chopped orange zest

3 cloves garlic, finely chopped

3 cups (6 oz/185 g) fresh white bread crumbs (page 17)

CRANBERRY SAUCE WITH CIDER AND CINNAMON

2 cups (16 fl oz/500 ml) unfiltered apple cider

2 cups (1 lb/500 g) sugar

¼ cup (2 fl oz/60 ml) water

1 cinnamon stick, 3 inches (7.5 cm) long

2 bags (12 oz/375 g each) fresh cranberries

In a medium-large nonaluminum saucepan, combine the apple cider, sugar, water, and cinnamon stick. Place over medium heat and bring to a simmer, stirring to dissolve the sugar. Add the cranberries, bring to a simmer, and cook, stirring occasionally, until most of the cranberries have burst, about 10 minutes.

Let cool to room temperature. Transfer to a bowl, cover, and refrigerate for at least 24 hours to develop the flavors. Remove the cinnamon stick and let the sauce come to room temperature before serving.

Make-Ahead Tip: The sauce must be prepared at least 24 hours in advance and can be prepared up to 3 days in advance.

MAKES 8–10 SERVINGS

CRANBERRIES

Growing on low bushes, often in bogs, cranberries are native to America and were enthusiastically adopted by early European colonists. The berries freeze well, but before the advent of refrigeration they were kept fresh in tubs of water. The quality of the berries was once measured by whether or not they bounced when dropped down a flight of stairs—a test that resulted in the alternative name of bounceberries.

CRANBERRY RELISH WITH GINGER

Cut the orange (with its peel on) into 16 chunks and discard any seeds. Working in batches, combine the orange chunks, cranberries, sugar, and ginger in a food processor. Pulse to chop finely and evenly, stopping once or twice with each batch to scrape down the sides of the work bowl.

Transfer to a storage container, cover, and refrigerate for at least 24 hours to develop the flavors. Bring to room temperature and stir well before serving.

Make-Ahead Tip: This relish improves when made in advance, since the flavors have more time to marry. Prepare it up to 3 days before serving.

MAKES 8–10 SERVINGS

1 orange, unpeeled and preferably organic, scrubbed

2 bags (12 oz/375 g each) fresh cranberries

1½ cups (12 oz/375 g) sugar

⅓ cup (2 oz/60 g) peeled and finely chopped fresh ginger

FRESH GINGER

The lively, clean flavor of fresh ginger is compatible with most fruits. In the market, look for ginger that is hard and heavy, with an unbroken peel that is thin, light colored, smooth, and shiny. To prepare ginger, peel it with a vegetable peeler or paring knife before using as directed in a recipe.

CARAMELIZED RED ONION RELISH

½ cup (4 oz/125 g)
unsalted butter

8 lb (4 kg) red onions
(about 10 large), halved
and thinly sliced

Salt and freshly ground
pepper

⅓ cup (2½ oz/75 g) firmly
packed golden brown
sugar

⅓ cup (3 fl oz/80 ml)
crème de cassis *(far right)*

⅓ cup (3 fl oz/80 ml) red
wine vinegar

1 tablespoon minced fresh
thyme or 1½ teaspoons
dried

In a very large frying pan over medium heat, melt half the butter. Add half of the onions and 1 teaspoon salt, cover, and cook, stirring occasionally, until the onions are tender and have rendered some of their liquid, about 15 minutes. Transfer to a bowl. Repeat with the remaining butter, onions, and 1 teaspoon salt.

Return the first batch of onions and any juices from their bowl to the frying pan. Stir in the brown sugar and cassis, and then add the vinegar. Cook over low heat, stirring and tossing frequently, until the onion juices have evaporated, about 30 minutes. Continue to cook uncovered, stirring occasionally, until the onions are tender and lightly browned, another 20–30 minutes.

Stir in the thyme and pepper to taste. Taste and adjust the salt. Serve hot.

Make-Ahead Tip: The relish can be prepared up to 3 days in advance of serving. Let cool, cover, and refrigerate, rewarming it over low heat just before serving.

MAKES 8–10 SERVINGS

CRÈME DE CASSIS
The tart-sweet quality of
crème de cassis, or black
currant liqueur, reinforces the
sweetness of the onions as
they brown, while its purple-
red color boosts the natural
hue of the onions. Once
opened, a bottle of cassis
will keep for many months
and is a nice addition to
both pantry and bar.
A nonalcoholic version of
cassis is also available.

POTATOES ON THE SIDE

Thanksgiving is a meal made up of traditional must-have foods, and no menu items are more crucial than the potato side dishes. You'll probably want mashed, to cozy up to the turkey under a shared ladle of gravy, and there should also be sweet potatoes or yams to provide golden contrast.

CLASSIC MASHED POTATOES
82

GOLDEN MASHED POTATOES WITH
LEEKS AND SOUR CREAM
85

RED POTATOES WITH BACON
86

CANDIED YAMS
89

TWO-POTATO GRATIN WITH CHEESE
90

CLASSIC MASHED POTATOES

Put the potatoes in a large saucepan and add water to cover. Salt the water, bring to a boil over medium heat, cover partially, and cook, stirring once or twice, until the potatoes are very tender, about 40 minutes. Drain.

Return the potatoes to the pan and place the pan over low heat. With a potato masher, mash the potatoes thoroughly. With a wooden spoon, fold the butter into the potatoes 1 tablespoon at a time, stirring briskly after each addition. Gradually stir in the hot milk. Stir in ½ teaspoon salt and 1 teaspoon pepper. Still using the wooden spoon, stir the potatoes until they are light and fluffy.

Remove the pan from the heat. Taste and adjust the seasoning with salt and pepper. Serve hot.

Make-Ahead Tip: Mashed potatoes are at their best when served right after they're mashed, but the potatoes can be peeled and held in a pan of cold water to cover for up to 1 hour before cooking.

MAKES 8–10 SERVINGS

5 lb (2.5 kg) russet potatoes, peeled and cut into large, uniform chunks

Salt and freshly ground pepper

½ cup (4 oz/125 g) unsalted butter, at room temperature

1⅔ cups (13 fl oz/405 ml) milk, heated to a simmer

MASHED POTATO TIPS

The best potatoes for mashing are those with the most starch, russet potatoes, since they beat into light, fluffy peaks. Cook off any excess moisture and dry the potatoes out (the better to absorb the milk and butter) by mashing them over low heat. A food mill or a ricer can be used in place of the masher, if wished, but potatoes should never be mashed in a food processor, for its powerful motor will make the potatoes gluey.

GOLDEN MASHED POTATOES WITH LEEKS AND SOUR CREAM

4 lb (2 kg) large Yukon gold potatoes, unpeeled and preferably organic, scrubbed

Salt and freshly ground pepper

½ cup (4 oz/125 g) unsalted butter

4 leeks, including tender green parts, finely chopped and well rinsed

1 cup (8 oz/250 g) sour cream, at room temperature

1 cup (8 fl oz/250 ml) milk, heated to a simmer

Cut the potatoes (with their peels on) into large, uniform chunks. Put the potato chunks in a large saucepan and add water to cover and a generous pinch of salt. Bring to a boil over medium heat, cover partially, and cook the potatoes, stirring once or twice, until the potatoes are very tender, about 40 minutes. Drain.

Meanwhile, in a frying pan over medium heat, melt the butter. Add the leeks, cover, and cook, stirring once or twice, until tender and lightly browned, 12–15 minutes. Set aside and keep warm.

Return the potatoes to the saucepan and place the pan over low heat. With a potato masher, mash the potatoes thoroughly. Stir in the leeks and their buttery juices. Add the sour cream and stir well. Add the hot milk, ½ teaspoon salt, and 1 teaspoon pepper and stir vigorously until light and fluffy.

Remove the pan from the heat. Taste and adjust the seasoning with salt and pepper. Serve hot.

Note: Yukon gold potatoes, increasingly common in the market, have a beautiful golden flesh and a high starch content, making them ideal mashers. Russet potatoes can be substituted, although they should be peeled.

MAKES 8–10 SERVINGS

CLEANING LEEKS

Earthbound leeks collect grit between their many layers as they grow and need to be carefully cleaned. For this recipe, trim off the roots and the toughest of the green tops, leaving only the white and pale green parts. Finely chop, then soak in a bowl in 3 changes of water, letting the grit settle to the bottom each time and lifting off the floating leeks with a slotted spoon. Rinse once more in a strainer under running water, then pat dry and proceed as directed.

RED POTATOES WITH BACON

Put the potatoes in a large saucepan and add water to cover and a generous pinch of salt. Bring to a boil over high heat. Reduce the heat slightly, cover partially, and cook, stirring occasionally, until the potatoes are just tender, about 12 minutes. Drain. Spread the potatoes out in a single layer on a shallow baking pan and let cool to room temperature.

In a large, heavy frying pan, arrange the bacon slices without overlapping. Cook over medium-high heat, turning several times, until almost crisp, about 8 minutes. Transfer to paper towels to drain and cool. Discard all but 1 tablespoon of the bacon drippings from the pan and reserve the pan. When the bacon is cool, chop it fairly fine.

Place the frying pan over medium-high heat and add the butter to the drippings. When it has melted, add the potatoes and cook, stirring and rolling the potatoes in the pan, until they begin to crisp and brown, 5–7 minutes. Add the bacon, reduce the heat to medium-low, and cook until the bacon is hot and the potatoes are very crisp, 2–3 minutes. Season with ¼ teaspoon salt and ½ teaspoon pepper and toss well. Add the parsley and toss again.

Taste and adjust the seasoning. Serve hot.

MAKES 8–10 SERVINGS

3 lb (1.5 kg) small red-skinned potatoes

Salt and freshly ground pepper

8 slices thick-cut bacon

1 tablespoon unsalted butter

⅓ cup (½ oz/15 g) minced fresh flat-leaf (Italian) parsley

BACON
Potatoes accommodate many flavors, none more readily than that of bacon. When bacon is the smoky seasoning as well as a major ingredient, only the best will do, so try to purchase it from a good butcher. Apple wood–smoked bacon is sweetly flavorful; choose a thick-sliced one that won't shrivel away during cooking.

CANDIED YAMS

5 lb (2.5 kg) orange-fleshed yams such as Garnet (about 6 large)

¼ cup (2 oz/60 g) unsalted butter, cut into small pieces, plus extra for greasing

½ cup (3½ oz/105 g) firmly packed golden brown sugar

Salt and freshly ground pepper

1¾ cups (3 oz/90 g) miniature marshmallows (optional)

½ cup (4 fl oz/125 ml) fresh orange juice

Preheat the oven to 400°F (200°C). Prick the yams several times with a fork. Put them in the oven and bake until just tender, about 1¼ hours. Transfer the yams to a wire rack and let them cool to room temperature. Cover loosely and let stand overnight at room temperature to firm their texture.

Preheat the oven to 350°F (180°C). Choose a 9-by-13-inch (23-by-33-cm) baking dish and grease it well.

Peel the yams and cut them into slices ½ inch (12 mm) thick. Arrange the slices, overlapping them, in the prepared dish. Evenly sprinkle the brown sugar and butter pieces over the yams. Season lightly with salt. Tightly cover the dish with aluminum foil and bake until hot and steaming, about 25 minutes.

Uncover the dish. If using, scatter the marshmallows over the yams. Drizzle the orange juice over the dish. Return the dish to the oven and continue to bake, basting occasionally with the syrup that accumulates in the pan, until the marshmallows are melted and gooey, 15–20 minutes. Season generously with pepper. Serve hot.

Make-Ahead Tip: The yams should be baked a day or so in advance to allow them to cool and firm up before assembling the dish. The dish can be assembled, covered with aluminum foil, and held at room temperature for several hours before baking.

MAKES 8–10 SERVINGS

YAMS

Americans love to eat candied yams, but what Americans call yams are actually orange-fleshed sweet potatoes. The true yam belongs to a different plant species from the sweet potato and is an important crop around the world but rarely available in the United States. When shopping for "yams," look for those with the darkest skins and flesh and the most moisture. The vegetables should be firm and unblemished, without any breaks in the skin. Garnet variety is a good choice.

TWO-POTATO GRATIN WITH CHEESE

COMTÉ CHEESE

A sweetly nutty and delicious cheese, Comté is a washed rind cheese with holes. Made in the Jura region, it is the French version of the better-known Swiss Gruyère. Both are among the world's great eating and cooking cheeses, and either will work well in this dish. (So, too, will a good aged Swiss from Switzerland, although it will be a little subtler in flavor than the other two.) Look for Comté and Gruyère in well-stocked cheese shops.

Preheat the oven to 325°F (165°C). Generously grease a 9-by-13-inch (23-by-33-cm) baking dish.

In a very large bowl, stir together the half-and-half, cream, 2½ teaspoons salt, and 1¼ teaspoons pepper. Add the russet and sweet potatoes and toss to mix and coat evenly with the cream mixture. Layer about one-fourth of the potato slices in the prepared dish. Keep the slices evenly but randomly divided between russet and sweet potatoes and be sure the layer reaches to the edges of the dish. Evenly scatter about one-fourth of the cheeses over the potato layer. Repeat to make 3 more layers, pressing with your palm if necessary to fit all the potatoes in the dish and reserving a final sprinkling of cheese. Pour any cream mixture remaining in the bowl evenly over the potatoes. Sprinkle the remaining cheese evenly over all. Scatter the butter pieces evenly over the cheese.

Transfer to the oven and bake until the top of the gratin is browned, the cream has thickened and is bubbling, and a knife inserted into the center of the gratin meets little resistance, about 1 hour and 20 minutes. (The russet potatoes will remain slightly firmer than the sweet potatoes.)

Transfer the gratin to a rack and let rest for 10–15 minutes before serving.

Make-Ahead Tip: The gratin can be prepared completely several hours in advance and then reheated. Just before serving, cover with aluminum foil and reheat in a preheated 325°F (165°C) oven for about 30 minutes.

MAKES 8–10 SERVINGS

2 tablespoons unsalted butter, cut into small pieces, plus extra for greasing

1 cup (8 fl oz/250 ml) half-and-half (half cream)

1 cup (8 fl oz/250 ml) heavy (double) cream

Salt and freshly ground pepper

2½ lb (1.25 kg) russet potatoes, peeled and sliced into rounds ⅛ inch (3 mm) thick

2½ lb (1.25 kg) sweet potatoes, peeled and sliced into rounds ⅛ inch (3 mm) thick

½ lb (250 g) shredded Comté, Gruyère, or aged Swiss cheese

¼ lb (125 g) Parmesan or Manchego cheese, grated

DESSERTS

No matter how bountiful the feast, one Thanksgiving rule must be followed: Save room for dessert. The hearty desserts that follow truly embody the holiday's spirit of abundance—and a couple of unexpected conclusions will allow those with revolutionary instincts to shake things up a bit.

CREAMY PUMPKIN PIE

To make a pie crust from scratch, follow the recipe on page 116.

Position a rack in the lower third of the oven and preheat to 425°F (220°C). In a large bowl, whisk together the pumpkin purée, brown sugar, and cream cheese until smooth. Whisk in the eggs one at a time. Add the half-and-half, vanilla, ginger, the ½ teaspoon allspice, the cinnamon, cloves, and a pinch of salt and stir to combine. Pour the filling into the pie shell, using a glass pie dish if possible (see page 97).

Place the pie in the oven and bake for 15 minutes. Reduce the oven temperature to 350°F (180°C) and continue to bake until the filling is evenly but not firmly set, about 35 minutes longer, for a total baking time of about 50 minutes. Check the pie 10 minutes before it is ready, and cover the crust with a collar of aluminum foil if it is browning too fast.

Transfer to a wire rack and let cool to room temperature before serving. Cut the pie into wedges, top each wedge with whipped cream, if desired, and lightly dust with allspice.

Make-Ahead Tip: This pie is at its best the day it is baked, without ever having been refrigerated. Arrange your kitchen schedule so that you take the pie out of the oven just as you slide the turkey in.

MAKES 8 SERVINGS

FRESH PUMPKIN PURÉE

Making your own pumpkin purée is easy and produces a fresher-tasting pie. Use 1 large or 2 medium Sugar Pie or other eating (not field) pumpkins. Cut out the stem, quarter the pumpkin length-wise, and scoop out the seeds. In a preheated 400°F (200°C) oven, bake the quarters cut side down in a shallow roasting pan, with a little water in the bottom, until tender, about 1 hour. Let cool, scrape the flesh from the peels, and force it through a medium-mesh sieve or the medium disk of a food mill. Freeze any leftover purée for up to 2 months.

1 unbaked 10-inch (25-cm) prepared or homemade pie shell (page 116), chilled

1¾ cups (14 oz/440 g) homemade or canned pumpkin purée *(far left)*

¾ cup (6 oz/185 g) firmly packed golden brown sugar

⅔ cup (5 oz/155 g) cream cheese, at room temperature

3 eggs

1½ cups (12 fl oz/375 ml) half-and-half (half cream)

1 teaspoon vanilla extract (essence)

½ teaspoon ground ginger

½ teaspoon ground allspice, plus extra for garnish

¼ teaspoon ground cinnamon

⅛ teaspoon ground cloves

Salt

Unsweetened whipped cream for serving (page 101) (optional)

PECAN PIE

1 unbaked 9-inch (23-cm) prepared or homemade pie shell (page 116), chilled

3 eggs

¾ cup (7½ oz/235 g) dark corn syrup

⅔ cup (5 oz/155 g) firmly packed dark brown sugar

¼ cup (3 oz/90 g) unsulfured light molasses

¼ cup (2 oz/60 g) unsalted butter, melted and slightly cooled

1 tablespoon Kahlúa or other coffee-flavored liqueur

¼ teaspoon salt

1½ cups (6 oz/185 g) coarsely chopped pecans

Unsweetened whipped cream for serving (page 101) (optional)

To make a pie crust from scratch, follow the recipe on page 116.

Position a rack in the lower third of the oven and preheat to 350°F (180°C). In a large bowl, whisk the eggs. Add the corn syrup, brown sugar, molasses, butter, liqueur, and salt and whisk until the mixture is smooth.

Scatter the pecans evenly in the pie shell. Pour the egg mixture over the pecans.

Place the pie in the oven and bake until the top is browned and the filling is evenly but not firmly set, about 50 minutes. Check the pie after 40 minutes, and cover the crust with a collar of aluminum foil if the crust is browning too fast.

Remove the pie from the oven, place it on a wire rack, and let it cool completely before cutting. To serve, cut into wedges and top each wedge with a dollop of whipped cream if desired.

Note: This pie is good warm, but it is so soft and liquid right after baking that it is difficult to slice. The solution: Let the pie cool completely, cut it, then rewarm the individual slices in a 300°F (150°C) oven for 5–10 minutes just before serving.

MAKES 6–8 SERVINGS

PIE DISH OR PAN?

Pies like this one and the pumpkin pie on page 94, which have liquid fillings poured into uncooked shells, can become soggy on the bottom. Prevent this by using a glass pie dish. A clear glass dish allows heat to radiate directly through it, cooking the bottom more quickly. If you must use a metal pan or ceramic dish, preheat a baking sheet on an oven rack as you preheat the oven and place the pie directly on the sheet to help the pie's bottom bake.

LATTICE-TOPPED APPLE PIE

To make a pie crust and lattice from scratch, follow the recipe on page 116.

Preheat the oven to 400°F (200°C). In large bowl, stir together the apples, brown sugar, flour, lemon juice, and vanilla. Let stand at room temperature, stirring once or twice, for 20 minutes. Spoon the apples and all the juices from the bowl into the pie shell, mounding the fruit slightly. Dot the apples with the butter and cover with the lattice top. Sprinkle the granulated sugar over the lattice.

Place the pie in the oven and bake until the crust is crisp and golden and the filling is bubbling, about 1 hour.

Remove from the oven, place on a wire rack, and let cool for at least 30 minutes before serving. Serve the pie warm or at room temperature, topped with a slice of cheese or accompanied with a scoop of ice cream, if desired.

Make-Ahead Tip: The pie is best baked the day it is to be eaten. Plan to remove it from the oven just before the turkey goes in.

MAKES 8 SERVINGS

APPLES FOR COOKING

Apples fall roughly into three categories, based on how they can best be used. Sauce apples (such as Cortlands) melt tenderly into custardy morsels, turning into apple-sauce with little more than a brief simmer. Baking apples (such as Rome Beauties and Golden Delicious) hold their shape after up to an hour in the oven. The latter two could be used here, but try an all-purpose apple. With a texture when cooked that falls between tender and al dente, the ever-popular Granny Smith is ideal for apple pie.

1 unbaked 10-inch (25-cm) prepared or homemade pie shell and lattice top (page 116), chilled

3½ lb (1.75 kg) Granny Smith apples (about 7 large), peeled, cored, and cut into ½-inch (12-mm) chunks

1 cup (7 oz/220 g) firmly packed golden brown sugar

¼ cup (1½ oz/45 g) unbleached all-purpose (plain) flour

2 tablespoons fresh lemon juice

1 teaspoon vanilla extract (essence)

2 tablespoons unsalted butter, cut into small pieces

1 teaspoon granulated sugar

Sharp Cheddar cheese or Rum-Brandy Ice Cream (page 106) for serving (optional)

GINGER-PEAR TORTE

6 tablespoons (3 oz/90 g) unsalted butter, plus extra for greasing

5 eggs, at room temperature

⅔ cup (5 oz/155 g) granulated sugar

½ cup (2 oz/60 g) sifted unbleached all-purpose (plain) flour

1 teaspoon ground ginger

½ cup (2 oz/60 g) finely ground blanched almonds

1 cup (8 fl oz/250 ml) heavy (double) cream

1 teaspoon freshly grated nutmeg

2 ripe but firm Bartlett (Williams') pears, about 1 lb (500 g) total weight

1 tablespoon finely chopped crystallized ginger

3 tablespoons firmly packed golden brown sugar

1 tablespoon brandy

Confectioners' (icing) sugar for dusting

Preheat the oven to 350°F (180°C). Grease two 8-inch (20-cm) round cake pans. Line the bottom of each pan with parchment (baking) paper. Butter the parchment.

In a small saucepan over medium heat, melt 4 tablespoons (2 oz/60 g) of the butter. Set aside to cool slightly. Meanwhile, using an electric mixer, beat the eggs until blended. Gradually beat in the granulated sugar. Continue to beat until the mixture is pale yellow and a slowly dissolving ribbon forms when the beaters are lifted, 6–8 minutes. Combine the flour and ground ginger. Sift half of the flour mixture over the egg mixture and fold it in with a rubber spatula. Fold in half of the butter. Repeat with the remaining flour mixture and butter. Fold in the almonds.

Divide the batter between the prepared pans. Bake until the edges of the layers are golden and just beginning to pull away from the sides of the pans, 15–20 minutes. Remove from the oven, place on wire racks, and let cool for 10 minutes. Turn the layers out onto the racks, peel off the paper, and let cool completely.

Just before serving, in a deep bowl, beat the cream to soft peaks. Sprinkle the nutmeg over the cream and continue to beat to stiff peaks. Cover and refrigerate.

Place 1 cake layer, bottom side up, on a serving plate. Peel and core the pears and cut into ½-inch (12-mm) chunks. In a large frying pan over medium heat, melt the remaining 2 tablespoons butter. Add the pears and crystallized ginger and cook, stirring once or twice, for 2 minutes. Raise the heat to high, add the brown sugar and brandy, and cook, stirring often, until the liquid is reduced to a thick glaze, about 4 minutes. Spoon the pears over the cake layer on the plate. Top with the second layer. Dust the top with confectioners' sugar. Serve warm with the whipped cream.

MAKES 6–8 SERVINGS

WHIPPED CREAM

Freshly whipped cream is one of the rich delights of the Thanksgiving holiday. It's easy enough, if you know a couple of tricks. First, be sure the cream is fresh (check the sell-by date) and is not ultra-pasteurized; it will whip higher. Chill the cream well and beat it in a deep chilled bowl with a chilled whisk or electric mixer beaters. Beat just until soft or stiff peaks form, but do not overbeat, or the cream will turn into butter. Once whipped, the cream will hold for 30 minutes or so, covered, in the refrigerator.

DRIED-FRUIT COMPOTE WITH BOURBON AND CRÈME ANGLAISE

CUSTARD SAVVY

Made from milk or cream, eggs, and sugar and cooked on the stove top, crème anglaise is probably the best-known custard sauce. Always use a heavy saucepan over low heat and do not raise the heat to speed the thickening process, as it may cause curdling. "Tempering" the eggs, or very gradually stirring hot liquid into them to warm them up, also prevents curdling. Once the sauce thickens enough to coat the back of a spoon and leaves a clear track when a finger is drawn through it, it is ready to remove from the heat.

To make the crème anglaise, in a bowl, whisk together the egg yolks and sugar. In a heavy saucepan over medium heat, bring the half-and-half to a gentle simmer. Slowly and gradually whisk the hot half-and-half into the egg yolk mixture.

Return the mixture to the pan and place over low heat. Cook, stirring constantly, until the mixture thickens enough to coat the back of a spoon and leaves a clear track when a finger is drawn through it, about 6 minutes. Do not let the mixture boil.

Immediately transfer to a bowl and let cool to room temperature. Stir in the vanilla and salt. Cover the bowl with plastic wrap, pressing it directly onto the surface of the custard to prevent a skin from forming. Refrigerate for at least 2 hours or up to 3 days.

In a heavy, large nonaluminum pan, combine the water, bourbon, and sugar. Place the pan over medium heat and stir occasionally to dissolve the sugar. Using a vegetable peeler, remove the zest of the orange in several long strips; add them to the pan. When the liquid simmers, add the apricots and figs. Cover partially and let simmer, stirring gently once or twice, for 15 minutes. Add the prunes and cherries, re-cover partially, and simmer until all the fruits are tender but still hold their shape, 4–6 minutes. Stir in the lemon juice.

To serve, remove and discard the orange zest. Divide the fruit and its poaching liquid among individual dishes. Drizzle the crème anglaise around (not over) the fruit and serve immediately.

Make-Ahead Tip: The compote can be prepared up to 3 days in advance. Let it come to room temperature, then rewarm it over low heat, stirring gently, just before serving.

MAKES 8–10 SERVINGS

FOR THE CRÈME ANGLAISE:

5 egg yolks

⅓ cup (3 oz/90 g) sugar

2 cups (16 fl oz/500 ml) half-and-half (half cream)

1 tablespoon vanilla extract (essence)

Pinch of salt

5 cups (40 fl oz/1.25 l) water

¾ cup (6 fl oz/180 ml) bourbon

⅔ cup (5 oz/155 g) sugar

1 large orange, preferably organic

1¼ cups (8 oz/250 g) dried apricots

1¼ cups (8 oz/250 g) dried Black Mission or Calimyrna figs, halved

1¼ cups (8 oz/250 g) pitted prunes, halved

1 cup (5 oz/155 g) dried sweet cherries

2 tablespoons fresh lemon juice

STEAMED CRANBERRY PUDDING

¼ cup (2 oz/60 g) unsalted butter, at room temperature, plus extra for greasing

3 tablespoons granulated sugar, plus extra for dusting

1½ cups (6 oz/185 g) coarsely chopped fresh cranberries

1½ cups (7½ oz/235 g) unbleached all-purpose (plain) flour

1¼ teaspoons baking powder

½ teaspoon baking soda (bicarbonate of soda)

¼ teaspoon salt

½ cup (3½ oz/105 g) firmly packed golden brown sugar

¼ cup (3 oz/90 g) unsulfured light molasses

2 teaspoons minced orange zest

⅓ cup (3 fl oz/80 ml) buttermilk

Boiling water, as needed

Rum-Brandy Ice Cream (page 106) or vanilla ice cream, softened slightly if necessary, for serving

Generously grease the inside of a decorative 2-qt (2-l) steamed-pudding mold, including the lid. Make sure that the bottom of the mold is especially well greased. Dust the mold and its lid with granulated sugar, shaking out the excess.

In a medium bowl, combine the cranberries and the 3 table-spoons granulated sugar and let stand while preparing the batter.

Sift together the flour, baking powder, baking soda, and salt onto a piece of waxed paper.

In a large bowl, whisk together the ¼ cup butter, the brown sugar, the molasses, and the orange zest. Stir in the dry ingredients and the buttermilk and mix well. Fold in the cranberries and any juices from the bowl. Spoon the mixture into the prepared mold and top with the lid.

Place the mold on a wire rack inside a large, heavy pot and add boiling water to come halfway up the sides of the mold, creating a hot-water bath *(right)*. Place over medium-low heat, cover the pot, and cook, adding more boiling water as needed to maintain the original level, until the pudding pulls away from the sides of the mold and a knife inserted at the center comes out clean, about 1½ hours.

Transfer the pudding mold to a wire rack. Uncover and let the pudding rest in the mold for 15 minutes. Invert onto a plate. Serve warm, cut into wedges and accompanied with the ice cream.

Make-Ahead Tip: The pudding can be prepared 1 day in advance. Wrap in plastic wrap and refrigerate. Bring to room temperature, wrap in aluminum foil, and rewarm in a preheated 300°F (150°C) oven for 20 minutes before serving.

MAKES 6–8 SERVINGS

HOT-WATER BATH

A hot-water bath, classically called a *bain-marie,* is a simple and effective way to protect delicate foods—puddings, custards, some cakes—from the hot, dry heat of the stove top or oven, ensuring that they will come out moist, tender, and, in the case of custards, uncracked. The pudding mold or other container holding the food is simpy placed in a larger container, and boiling water is poured into the larger container to come halfway up the sides of the mold, creating an insulating layer of water to moderate the heat.

RUM-BRANDY ICE CREAM

In a bowl, whisk together the egg yolks, sugar, and nutmeg. In a heavy saucepan over medium heat, combine the half-and-half and cream and bring to a gentle simmer. Slowly and gradually whisk the hot cream mixture into the egg yolk mixture.

Return the mixture to the pan and place over low heat. Cook, stirring constantly, until the mixture thickens enough to coat the back of a metal spoon and leaves a clear track when a finger is drawn through it, about 4 minutes. Do not let the mixture boil.

Immediately transfer to a bowl and let cool to room temperature. Stir in the vanilla. Cover the bowl with plastic wrap, pressing it directly onto the surface of the custard to prevent a skin from forming. Refrigerate for at least 2 hours or preferably overnight.

Freeze in an ice-cream maker according to the manufacturer's instructions until softly frozen. Add the rum and the brandy and continue to churn until the ice cream freezes further. (Due to the alcohol content, it may not freeze solid.) Transfer to a storage container, cover, and place in the freezer overnight before serving.

Make-Ahead Tip: Ideally, the custard is refrigerated overnight and then the ice cream is frozen overnight, which means that the ice cream must be started 2 days in advance of serving. Alternatively, the custard can be refrigerated for only 2 hours. If necessary, soften the ice cream in the refrigerator for 10–15 minutes before scooping.

MAKES ABOUT 1½ QT (1.5 L)

4 egg yolks

⅔ cup (5 oz/155 g) sugar

½ teaspoon freshly grated nutmeg

2½ cups (20 fl oz/625 ml) half-and-half (half cream)

1½ cups (12 fl oz/375 ml) heavy (double) cream

1 teaspoon vanilla extract (essence)

2 tablespoons dark rum

2 tablespoons brandy

FREEZING ICE CREAM

To make a generous amount of ice cream, use an ice-cream maker, either an electric model or a hand-cranked one, with a dasher that is turned constantly to incorporate air into the custard as it freezes. A frozen-canister ice-cream maker, which is turned only every 15 minutes or so, will make a delicious, heavy ice cream but not enough volume to serve a large Thanksgiving crowd.

THANKSGIVING BASICS

Thanksgiving dinner is one of the most anticipated meals of the year. No other holiday captures the spirit of sharing a home-cooked feast with family and friends in quite the same heartwarming way. And, no other meal creates quite the same demands as those endured by the Thanksgiving cook. Careful planning in advance—and some helping hands in the kitchen—can ease the pressures of creating a memorable holiday and can help you spend more of your time visiting with family and friends.

SELECTING A MENU

Putting together a Thanksgiving menu to accommodate the tastes of all the guests on your list can be a challenging task. You'll want to select a well-matched combination of appetizers, main dishes, sides, and desserts that best suits the taste of your family and friends and the spirit of the celebration you want to host. For suggested menus, see page 119. If you decide to create your own menu, keep in mind that you will need to select recipes that offer a variety of colors, flavors, and textures and that vary in their need for last-minute attention.

ESTIMATING QUANTITIES

An impending Thanksgiving crowd can fool the cook into thinking that all the recipes must be doubled or tripled in order to have enough food for everyone. In truth, faced with the holiday's traditional large menu, most diners take a smaller-than-typical portion of each dish. For details on choosing the right-sized bird, see Choosing a Turkey, page 110.

GETTING ORGANIZED

Preparation and organization play key roles in ensuring an enjoyable holiday for the Thanksgiving cook. Read through all the recipes you are planning to make a week or two ahead of time and draw up shopping lists of any ingredients and equipment you need. Be sure to give yourself plenty of time in advance to buy everything, thereby avoiding the rush of shoppers and the risk of empty shelves at your market on the day before Thanksgiving. Finish cleaning house a day or two before Thanksgiving. The time you devote to planning will allow you to relax with your guests on the holiday.

It's also a good idea to complete as many steps in advance as possible in your recipes. Tasks like washing lettuce greens, chopping vegetables, or making salad dressing can be done the day before. Many first courses or side dishes, such as Butternut Squash Soup (page 18), Candied Yams (page 89), or Two-Potato Gratin with Cheese (page 90), can be prepared almost completely ahead of time and then reheated or baked just before serving. Other necessary items such as pie shells (page 116) and turkey stock (page 115) can be made and stored in the refrigerator or freezer for days—or sometimes weeks—before you plan to use them in a recipe.

Since Thanksgiving is a feast that typically ties up the oven with essentials like turkey, dressing, rolls, and pie, choose as many of your other side dishes as possible from among those that can be cooked on top of the stove, such as Green Beans with Pecans (page 67) or Maple-Glazed Carrots (page 64). You will avoid last-minute oven gridlock and stay cool in the kitchen. If you like to grill, try the Hickory-Smoked Turkey with Horseradish-Apple Sauce (page 40), which spends just a short time in the oven, freeing it up for other holiday dishes.

TURKEY BASICS

No matter how spectacular your hors d'oeuvres or how delicious your pie, the turkey will take center stage on Thanksgiving Day. A feat that cooks usually undertake only once a year, roasting a whole turkey can be intimidating. Whether you are a novice or an expert, the following tips will help you present the perfect bird.

CHOOSING A TURKEY

Fresh turkeys are easy to find during the holidays and taste immeasurably better than their frozen counterparts, which will have drier meat. If at all possible, choose a fresh bird that was raised free range and fed organic grain. These turkeys have more flavor than those raised on factory farms and can be ordered from specialty butchers or natural-foods stores. Avoid self-basting turkeys, which are injected with a yellow, fatty substance to keep them moist. This process is unnecessary when a bird is covered with damp cheesecloth (muslin) and basted regularly as it roasts. If you decide to choose a free-range, organic turkey, be sure to follow the turkey packer's tips for roasting, which usually accompany the bird. These turkeys may require different roasting techniques than do ordinary super-market varieties.

For the best results, buy a turkey that weighs more than 10 pounds (5 kg). If you want a smaller bird, a turkey breast is a better choice. When calculating how large a turkey you'll need, figure on ¾ pound (375 g) per person, although you will probably want twice that (or even more) for leftovers.

Plan to pick up a fresh turkey the day before it is to be roasted, and store it in its original wrapping in the coldest part of the refrigerator. Frozen turkeys should also be kept in the refrigerator as they thaw to keep bacteria from multiplying. Figure on 3–4 hours per pound (500 g) for turkey to thaw, and keep in mind that it may take 2–5 days for a frozen turkey to defrost completely. Thawed turkey should be cooked within 2 days and should not be refrozen, or the texture of the meat will suffer.

ROASTING HOW-TO

Producing juicy, succulent meat can be a challenge when roasting a bird in the dry heat of an oven. Among the secrets to well-browned turkey with moist meat are trussing it to keep its shape more compact, basting it regularly, and checking the internal temperature with an instant-read thermometer. Following is some helpful advice.

SELECTING THE PAN

For the best results, roast a turkey on a metal roasting rack set inside a sturdy, shallow roasting pan. Using a heavy roasting pan will help keep the pan juices from burning. Don't use a pan with a nonstick surface; a regular surface allows more brown bits to stick to the pan during roasting, which results in tastier gravy. If you must use a disposable foil pan, buy 2 and double up for extra strength.

A metal roasting rack will keep the bottom of the turkey from stewing in the pan drippings and sticking to the pan. It also helps to produce clearer pan drippings, which means a better gravy. You can use a wire cake rack in a pinch, but a V-shaped nonstick roasting rack is best, as it elevates the food and allows more of its surface to brown. It also makes removing the turkey from the pan less cumbersome.

The turkey will be easier to handle if the pan is proportional to the bird's size. For a turkey weighing 10–14 pounds (5–7 kg), use a pan measuring 14 by 10 by 2½ inches (35 by 25 by 6 cm); for 16–20 pounds (8–10 kg), use a pan measuring 17 by 11½ by 2½ inches (43 by 29 by 6 cm); for 24 pounds (12 kg) and over, use a pan measuring 19 by 14 by 3¼ inches (48 by 35 by 8.5 cm).

PREPARING THE BIRD

Check the turkey's body cavities for the neck and giblets. Remove and reserve for use as directed in the recipe you have chosen. Rinse the turkey inside and out and pat it dry. Remove and discard any large pieces of fat from the cavities and trim off and discard excess fat on the outside of the turkey. Lightly season the turkey inside and out with salt and freshly ground pepper.

STUFFING THE BIRD

Roasting a bird unstuffed, with a dressing baked separately, saves time and effort—and results in a more evenly cooked bird. A dressing cooked in a baking dish contains none of the additional fat that it would absorb inside the turkey. But for many, a stuffed bird is Thanksgiving tradition. The stuffing baked in a bird is always more moist and more delicious than dressing baked separately, as its flavor improves with the added fat.

If you decide to stuff your turkey, finish making the stuffing just before roasting. This way, the warm stuffing can be put into the bird and then directly into the oven. If you make the stuffing in advance, be sure to warm it up before filling the bird. This gives the stuffing a good start in cooking, helping ensure that it will be fully cooked when the turkey is done. Use a large spoon or your hands to loosely stuff the body and neck cavities. Do not pack it tightly, as the stuffing will expand while the turkey roasts. Truss the main cavity *(see below)* to hold the stuffing inside the bird.

Stuffing must also be tested for doneness. To be safe to eat, it must register an internal temperature of 165°F (74°C) on an instant-read thermometer. (If it is not done when the bird is, transfer the stuffing to a buttered baking dish and continue to bake until it tests done.) Remove all of the stuffing at serving time and transfer it to a warmed dish. Do not let the stuffing sit for more than 2 hours in the roasted turkey.

TRUSSING THE BIRD

Trussing, or tying, a whole bird into a compact shape yields a roast turkey with a plump, tidy form that makes an attractive presentation at the table. A trussed turkey is also neater and easier to carve. But trussing is mainly a matter of looks: an untrussed bird may cook more evenly.

If you decide to truss, use a good, sturdy linen kitchen string, which is less likely than cotton to scorch in the oven. If you are roasting a turkey that has been stuffed, secure the stuffing by passing several trussing pins through the skin on both sides of the main cavity. Cut a generous length of kitchen string and, starting at the topmost pin, interlace the string back and forth as you would shoelaces. Pull it snug and tie it securely at the bottom.

To secure the drumsticks, cut a piece of string about 10 inches (25 cm) long. Transfer the turkey to a rack in a roasting pan and cross the drumsticks. Wind the string around the drumsticks and tie the ends together tightly.

Tuck the first joint of each wing under the second joint. This should be done when roasting any bird, whether or not you truss it, because it keeps the wing tips from becoming overly browned.

BASTING

Contrary to popular belief, basting does not add moisture to poultry or meat, but basting will help slow the turkey's drying out as it cooks and will give the skin rich color. A good rule of thumb is to begin basting the turkey after about 30 minutes of roasting and to baste every 30 minutes thereafter until the turkey is done. Use a bulb baster or large spoon to collect the pan juices and pour them evenly over the entire bird. Since the oven door is open while you baste, work quickly to minimize the heat lost each time. (See also Basting Savvy, page 28.)

ROASTING TIMES AND TEMPERATURES

Basting will help keep the surface of a roasted turkey from drying out too quickly, but nothing will keep a turkey's meat juicy if you overcook it. Paying attention to the internal temperature while roasting is the only guarantee of a delicious, moist, succulent turkey.

First, bring the turkey as close as possible to room temperature. Remove it from the refrigerator 2 hours before roasting, but no longer. This is the maximum time allowed for food safety.

For an unstuffed bird, figure on a roasting time of 15–20 minutes per pound (500 g) for 10- to 15-pound (5- to 7.5-kg) birds and 13–15 minutes per pound for birds over 16 pounds (8 kg). If the turkey is stuffed, add at least 30 minutes to the total cooking time for a bird up to 16 pounds (8 kg), or up to 1 hour for a larger turkey. This timing is based on roasting the turkey at a temperature of 325°F (165°C). Roasting at this temperature will prevent the outer section of the bird from overcooking before the center has finished cooking.

TESTING FOR DONENESS

About 30 minutes before the turkey is supposed to come out of the oven, insert an instant-read thermometer into the thickest part of the thigh without touching the bone (bone conducts heat, skewing the reading). Note that the internal temperature of meat must reach a minimum of 160°F (71°C) in order to destroy any food-borne bacteria. The temperature of the thigh should reach 175°F (80°C). Do not leave the thermometer in the turkey while it roasts. The breast will be done before the thigh; if it appears to be in danger of overbrowning during the final minutes of roasting, cover it with aluminum foil. Place the foil shiny side out to deflect the heat.

Because heat is trapped inside the turkey, it will continue to cook after you remove it from the oven. Take it out when the temperature is 3–4°F (1–2°C) below the temperatures given above to prevent it from overcooking and thus drying out. Transfer the turkey to a carving board, cover loosely with aluminum foil, and let rest for at least 20 minutes before carving. An uncarved 13-pound (6.5-kg) turkey will stay hot for up to an hour after removing it from the oven, giving you time to cook dressing, yams, and other dishes that need to be baked just before serving.

FOOD SAFETY TIPS

Following are a few precautions and safety tips to keep in mind when preparing the Thanksgiving meal.

Make sure your refrigerator is cold enough. A refrigerator thermometer placed on the top shelf should read no higher than 40°F (4°C).

Make sure that your turkey is not leaking in your refrigerator. If needed, place it on a rimmed tray and store it in two plastic bags, so that its juices won't contaminate other food.

Let large quantities of hot food cool before putting them into the refrigerator; otherwise, the hot food can lower the internal temperature of the refrigerator, compromising the safety of the other food stored there.

Before and after you handle any ingredient, especially raw turkey, wash your hands thoroughly with warm water and lots of soap.

Use separate cutting boards for animal products and for produce. And, always be sure to thoroughly wash any cutting surfaces, dishware, cookware, and kitchen tools that also came in contact with the raw food.

Do not let perishables sit out of the refrigerator for more than 2 hours. Never put stuffing into a turkey the day before (or even several hours before) roasting. Warm food can be hospitable to breeding bacteria.

CARVING A TURKEY

Use a good, sharp carving knife and a two-pronged fork for carving. Begin carving on one side of the turkey and completely carve this side before moving to the other. Shown opposite are the basic steps.

1 Removing the wing: Pull the wing away from the body and slice through the skin to locate the shoulder joint. Cut through the joint to remove the wing.

2 Removing the whole leg: Set the turkey breast side up. Pull the leg away from the body and slice through the skin to locate the thigh joint. Cut through the joint to remove the entire leg.

3 Separating the thigh and leg: Cut through the joint that separates the drumstick from the thigh. Serve these pieces whole, or carve them by cutting off the meat in thin slices parallel to the bone.

4 Carving the breast: Just above the thigh and shoulder joints, carve a deep horizontal cut through the breast toward the bone to create a base cut. Starting near the breastbone, carve thin slices vertically, cutting downward to end each slice at the base cut.

MAKING GRAVY

Simply and quickly prepared from the juices left in the roasting pan, gravy is an essential part of the Thanksgiving turkey and its accompaniments.

1 Deglazing the pan: After removing the turkey from the roasting pan, place the pan across 2 burners and turn them to medium-high. Add liquid to the pan and bring to a brisk simmer. Stir to deglaze the pan, scraping up the browned bits from the bottom.

2 Straining the gravy: Pour the contents of the pan through a sieve set over a bowl, pressing on the solids with the back of a spoon to extract all the liquid; discard the solids.

3 Degreasing the gravy: Using a large, flat spoon, skim off and discard the layer of fat that floats to the surface, or pour the liquid into a fat separator and pour off the liquid.

4 Thickening the gravy: Transfer the liquid to a saucepan, place over medium-high heat, and simmer briskly. In a small bowl, stir together a little stock or other liquid and some cornstarch (cornflour). Gradually stir this mixture into the simmering liquid. Cook for a few minutes, until the gravy thickens. Add salt and freshly ground pepper to taste.

TURKEY STOCK

3 tablespoons peanut oil

2 turkey wing drumettes (page 120)

Turkey neck, heart, and gizzard (optional)

3 cups (15 oz/470 g) chopped yellow onion

2 cups (10 oz/315 g) chopped carrot

1 cup (5 oz/155 g) chopped celery

Stems from 1 bunch fresh parsley

2 fresh thyme sprigs or 2 teaspoons dried

2 bay leaves

8 cups (64 fl oz/2 l) low-sodium canned chicken broth

¾ cup (6 fl oz/180 ml) dry white wine, dry sherry, or tawny Port

Salt and freshly ground pepper

Warm the oil in a stockpot over medium-high heat. Brown the turkey well, turning once or twice, about 14 minutes. Stir in the vegetables and herbs. Reduce the heat to low, cover, and cook, scraping the browned bits from the bottom of the pot occasionally, about 15 minutes. (If making giblet gravy, remove the heart and gizzard at this point and reserve.) Add the broth, wine, and salt and pepper to taste and bring to a simmer. Cover partially and cook for 35 minutes.

Strain the stock, pouring it through a sieve into a large bowl. If using right away, spoon off the visible fat or pour into a fat separator. Otherwise, let cool for about 30 minutes, then cover and refrigerate for a few hours or overnight. Using a large spoon, remove the solid fat from the top of the stock and discard. Refrigerate for up to 3 days or freeze for up to 3 months. Makes about 7 cups (56 fl oz/1.75 l).

PIE SHELLS

FOR ONE 9- OR 10-INCH (23- OR 25-CM)
PIE SHELL:

**2¼ cups (11½ oz/360 g) unbleached
all-purpose (plain) flour**

Pinch of salt

**7 tablespoons (3½ oz/105 g) cold unsalted
butter, cut into ½-inch (12-mm) pieces**

**⅓ cup (2½ oz/75 g) vegetable shortening,
frozen, cut into ½-inch (12-mm) pieces**

**About 8 tablespoons (4 fl oz/125 ml) ice
water**

FOR ONE 10-INCH (25-CM) PIE SHELL PLUS
LATTICE TOP:

**3⅔ cups (19 oz/590 g) unbleached
all-purpose (plain) flour**

¼ teaspoon salt

**10 tablespoons (5 oz/155 g) cold unsalted
butter, cut into ½-inch (12-mm) pieces**

**½ cup (4 oz/125 g) vegetable shortening,
frozen, cut into ½-inch (12-mm) pieces**

**About 12 tablespoons (6 fl oz/180 ml) ice
water**

In a food processor, combine the flour and
salt and pulse to blend. Add the butter and
shortening and pulse 5 or 6 times, until the
mixture is the texture of coarse meal with
some pea-sized bits. Add the water a little at
a time through the feed tube, pulsing once
after each addition, adding just enough to
make a moist but crumbly dough; it will not
hold together on its own but only when
gathered into a ball with your hands.

Turn the dough out onto a lightly floured
surface. For one pie shell only, gather the
dough into a ball and flatten into a thick
disk. For a pie shell plus a lattice top, gather
about two-thirds of the dough into one ball
(for the shell) and the remaining one-third
into a smaller ball (for the top), then flatten
into thick disks. Wrap in plastic wrap and
refrigerate for at least 1 hour or up to
overnight.

If the dough is very cold and hard, let it
stand, still wrapped, at room temperature
for 15 minutes. To make a pie shell, unwrap
the disk of dough and place it on a floured
surface. Lightly flour the top of the dough.
With a rolling pin, gently flatten the dough
into a rough round. Begin rolling out the
dough, always rolling straight away from
you and giving the round a quarter turn
every 2 or 3 rolls. If the dough sticks to the
work surface, release it with a spatula and
lightly flour beneath it. Lightly flour the top
of the dough if it begins sticking to your
rolling pin.

When the dough round is about ¼ inch
(6 mm) thick and about 2 inches (5 cm)
wider than your pie plate, roll it up around
the rolling pin, then unroll it into the pie
dish, centering it. Ease the dough into the
dish without stretching it. Trim the edges,
leaving about a 1-inch (2.5-cm) overhang.

To make a single-crust pie, fold the overhang
underneath itself and flute it decoratively.
Refrigerate the pie shell for at least
30 minutes, or wrap it carefully in plastic
wrap and refrigerate for up to 24 hours. Fill
and bake the chilled shell as directed in
individual recipes.

For a lattice-top pie, leave the trimmed
overhang until you are done preparing the
lattice (instructions follow). Shown opposite
are the basic steps in making a lattice top:

Roll out the smaller disk of dough into a
rectangle about 5 by 11 inches (13 by 28 cm).
Cut the pastry into 10 strips, each ½ inch
(12 mm) wide and 11 inches (28 cm) long.

1 Lay 5 of the strips across the filled pie
shell horizontally. Think of the top strip as
number 1, the bottom strip as number 5.

2 Fold strips 2 and 4 back onto themselves
to your left. Lay a vertical strip down the
center of the pie. Unfold strips 2 and 4.

3 Fold strips 1, 3, and 5 onto themselves to
your left. Lay a vertical strip to the right of
the center strip. Unfold strips 1, 3, and 5.

4 Fold strips 1, 3, and 5 onto themselves
to your right. Lay a vertical strip to the left of
the center strip. Unfold strips 1, 3, and 5.

If the lattice seems too open, add the last
2 strips to the right and left sides of the pie
in the same manner.

Fold the crust and lattice underneath themselves and use a fork to crimp, pressing and
sealing together the lattice and bottom crust.

SUGGESTED MENUS

Most American families have a set Thanksgiving menu that varies little from year to year. It is often a mixture of very traditional dishes and sometimes offbeat family favorites. If a fresh approach is desired, the menus that follow—blending the old and the new—will provide the cook with inspiration. When planning any menu, be sure to read through the recipes well ahead of time to plan out how to coordinate the timing of the cooking.

A NEW ENGLAND THANKSGIVING

Sherried Shrimp Bisque

Classic Roast Turkey
with Giblet Gravy
Classic Mashed Potatoes
Bread Dressing with Celery
Brussels Sprouts
in White Cheddar Sauce
Maple-Glazed Carrots

Steamed Cranberry Pudding with
Rum-Brandy Ice Cream

AN ELEGANT THANKSGIVING

Curried Nuts and Raisins
Watercress, Endive, and Pear Salad

Brined Turkey Breast
with Lemon-Parsley Gravy
Braised Chestnuts with Madeira
Cream Sauce
Red Potatoes with Bacon
Cranberry Relish with Ginger

Dried-Fruit Compote
with Bourbon and Crème Anglaise

A TRADITIONAL THANKSGIVING

Spicy Three-Cheese Spread

Classic Roast Turkey
with Giblet Gravy
Bread Dressing with Celery
Green Beans with Pecans
Classic Mashed Potatoes
Candied Yams
Cranberry Sauce
with Cider and Cinnamon
Poppy-Seed Cloverleaf Rolls

Creamy Pumpkin Pie

A FARMSTEAD THANKSGIVING

Butternut Squash Soup

Baked Ham
with Honey-Brandy Glaze
Broccoli with a Crunchy
Crumb Topping
Two-Potato Gratin with Cheese
Buttermilk Corn Bread or
Sweet Potato Biscuits
Cranberry Sauce
with Cider and Cinnamon

Lattice-Topped Apple Pie

A SOUTHERN THANKSGIVING

Mixed Greens
with Bacon-Wrapped Figs

Hickory-Smoked Turkey
with Horseradish-Apple Sauce
Corn Bread Dressing
with Oysters and Ham
Candied Yams
Cranberry Sauce
with Cider and Cinnamon
Buttermilk Corn Bread

Pecan Pie

GLOSSARY

BARTLETT PEARS Also called Williams' pears, Bartletts are medium sized and shaped roughly like bells. They have thin green skins that ripen to creamy yellow, sometimes tinged with red. Their slightly musky aromatic flesh is very soft and juicy when ripe, and their fine texture and mild taste make them good both for eating out of hand and for cooking.

BELGIAN ENDIVE Also known as endive or witloof, this member of the chicory family is widely grown in Belgium. The plant's roots are forced to sprout in darkened, humid rooms, which yields small, white (or sometimes red-tipped), tightly furled, bullet-shaped heads. Belgian endive is fragile and should be handled with care.

BELL PEPPERS Sweet-fleshed, bell-shaped members of the pepper family, bell peppers are also known as sweet peppers or capsicums. Green bell peppers are usually more sharply flavored than red ones, the latter being simply a sweeter and more mature stage of the former. Orange and yellow bell peppers are separate varieties.

BOURBON This slightly sweet whiskey takes its name from a county in Kentucky and is made from fermented grain, primarily corn. Straight bourbon must be at least 51 percent corn.

BULB BASTER Also called a turkey baster, this plastic, glass, or metal tube with a squeezable bulb at one end helps distribute liquid from the pan over the meat while it is roasting. Metal or glass basters will last longer than plastic ones, which can be warped or melted by the hot fat.

BUTTERMILK A form of cultured lowfat or nonfat milk in which the sugars have turned to acids, buttermilk adds a tangy flavor and thick, creamy texture to batters and doughs. Its acidity also adds a boost to the chemical leavening agents, baking powder and baking soda, adding extra lightness.

BUTTERNUT SQUASH Sometimes a foot (30 cm) long or longer, with beige skin and orange-yellow flesh, a butternut squash is identifiable by the round bulb at one end. It has flavorful, dense flesh and is especially good for baking and puréeing.

CAYENNE PEPPER A very hot ground red pepper made from dried cayenne and other chiles, cayenne is used quite sparingly in a wide variety of recipes to add heat or heighten flavor. Because different blends vary in heat, and because only a little is needed, always begin with a small amount and add more to taste in tiny increments.

CHEDDAR CHEESE A cow's milk cheese appreciated for its sharp, salty flavor, which ranges from mild to sharp. Farmhouse Cheddars taste stronger than other American Cheddars.

CHIMNEY STARTER A sheet-metal cylinder that is used to start charcoal without the use of lighter fluid. The chimney is placed on a grill's bottom grate, then stuffed with crumpled newspaper and charcoal. The newspaper is lit, and in as little as 20 minutes the coals will be covered with a white ash and ready for grilling.

CORN SYRUP Made from cornstarch, corn syrup is used to sweeten everything from commercial candies and jams to home-baked goods. It comes in dark and light versions. Corn syrup does not crystallize when heated, which is a boon for candy making. It also adds moisture and chewiness to cakes and cookies. Dark corn syrup has more flavor than light syrup.

DRUMETTES The meatiest sections of a turkey's wings, drumettes give plenty of flavor to stock. Buy them in any super-market meat department and freeze them for up to 3 months until needed.

EGGS, SEPARATING When separating egg whites from egg yolks, start with cold eggs, which separate more easily than room-temperature eggs. Position 2 bowls side by side. Crack the egg sharply on its equator, making a clean break, and pour the yolk and whites into your clean, cupped hand, letting the whites run through your fingers into one of the bowls and depositing the yolk in the other. You can also use an egg separator, a small bowl-shaped device with a depression made to hold the yolk while the white slips through. Or, pass the egg back and forth from one shell half to the other. Be careful not to let any yolk get into the whites, or the whites will not beat properly.

FAT SEPARATOR Sometimes called a degreasing pitcher, a fat separator is shaped like a measuring cup but has a spout that begins at the base of the cup. When liquid is added to the cup, the fat rises to the top, allowing the stock or other pan juices to be poured out through the spout, leaving the fat behind in the cup.

FENNEL Also known as sweet fennel or finocchio, a fennel plant's leaves, seeds, and stems have a sweet, faint aniselike flavor. Similar in appearance and texture to celery, fennel has stems that overlap at the base to form a somewhat flat bulb with white to pale green ribbed layers. The leaves are light and feathery.

FIGS Soft, pear-shaped figs with their many tiny seeds are actually swollen flowers turned in on themselves. Among the best-known varieties are the small, dark purple, sweet-tasting Mission or Black Mission and the gold-skinned Calimyrna. When dried, figs become even sweeter and delightfully chewy.

FOLDING A method used to combine two ingredients or mixtures with different densities, folding is a simple but crucial technique. Light, airy mixtures such as egg whites or whipped cream will lose their loft if incorrectly folded into heavier batters. To fold, spoon one-fourth of the lighter mixture atop the heavier mixture. With a long-handled rubber spatula, slice down through both mixtures and sweep the spatula along the bottom of the bowl. Bring the spatula with a gentle circular motion up and over the contents, lifting up some of the heavier batter from the bottom of the bowl over the top of the lighter mixture without deflating the lighter mixture. Rotate the pan or bowl a quarter turn and repeat the down-across-up-over motion. Continue, rotating the bowl each time, until the lighter mixture is incorporated. Don't overmix, as overmixing will deflate the lighter mixture.

GIBLETS A term referring to the heart, gizzard, and liver of a turkey or other poultry. In a purchased bird, the giblets, along with the neck, often are placed in a small paper package and stuffed inside the cavity. They make a nice addition to gravy and to dressing or stuffing.

GINGER, CRYSTALLIZED Ginger that has been candied in sugar syrup and then coated with granulated sugar. It adds sweet-spicy flavor to dessert fruit fillings, baked goods, and salads.

GORGONZOLA CHEESE A cow's milk blue cheese from northern Italy with a moist, creamy texture and complex flavor. It may be labeled *dolce* or *naturale*, the former a younger and milder version and the latter aged, stronger tasting, and more aromatic.

HICKORY CHIPS Chips of aromatic hickory wood are typically soaked in water and then added to glowing coals to infuse the cooking food with their fragrant smoke.

HONEY The natural, sweet, syruplike substance produced by bees from flower nectar, honey subtly reflects the color, taste, and aroma of the blossoms from which it was made. Milder varieties, such as clover and orange blossom, are the best choices for general cooking.

INSTANT-READ THERMOMETER Inserted near the end of cooking, instant-read thermometers are more accurate and make smaller holes in the meat, and thus release fewer juices, than other types of thermometers. When testing for doneness, be sure the thermometer is not touching a bone, and do not leave the thermometer in the turkey while it is still roasting in the oven.

LEEKS A sweet and moderately flavored member of the onion family, a leek is long and cylindrical with a pale white root end and dark green leaves. Select firm, unblemished leeks, small to medium in size. Grown in sandy soil, the leafy-topped multilayered vegetables require thorough cleaning (see page 85).

LIMA BEANS Lima beans grow in wide, flat inedible green pods. The inner seed, the sweet-tasting edible portion, should be as green as possible. Limas are also known as butter beans.

MADEIRA A fortified wine from the Portuguese island of the same name, Madeira ranges in flavor and color from light, nutty, and dry aperitif wines to darker, sweet after-dinner varieties.

MANCHEGO CHEESE Manchego is made in the Spanish region of La Mancha from milk produced by the many sheep in the area. The cheese has a tangy, almost nutty flavor, firm texture, and lovely ivory to pale gold color. Its rind, which can range from yellow to greenish black, is covered with a braided pattern. In Spain, Manchego is a favorite tapa, or small dish, served on its own with sherry or red wine. Italian pecorino romano can be substituted.

MOLASSES A thick, robust-tasting syrup, molasses is a by-product of cane sugar refining. Each step in the molasses-making process produces a different type of molasses. Mixed with pure cane syrup, light molasses has the lightest flavor and color. Dark molasses is thicker, darker, stronger in flavor, and less sweet than light molasses. Both light and dark molasses may be bleached with sulfur dioxide. Processed without sulfur, unsulfured molasses has a milder flavor. Molasses gives a distinctive flavor to many sweet and savory baked foods.

MUSHROOMS

Cremini: Common brown mushrooms, cremini are closely related to common white mushrooms and can be used whenever white mushrooms are called for. They have a firmer texture and fuller flavor. Fully mature cremini are known as portobello mushrooms.

Shiitake: Meaty in flavor, these Asian mushrooms have flat, dark brown caps usually 2–3 inches (5–7.5 cm) wide. They are available fresh or dried.

MUSTARD, DIJON True Dijon mustard is made in Dijon, France, from dark brown mustard seeds (unless marked blanc), white wine or wine vinegar, and herbs. Silky smooth and fairly hot and sharp tasting, Dijon mustard and non-French blends labeled Dijon style are widely available in supermarkets.

NUTS

Cashews: Kidney-shaped, crisp nuts with a slightly sweet and buttery flavor, cashews are native to Africa and India.

Chestnuts: Known as *marrons* in France, chestnuts are large and wrinkled and have a smooth, shiny, mahogany-colored shell shaped like a turban, but slightly flat on one side. They are often treated like a vegetable and are almost always cooked. (See also page 71.)

Hazelnuts: See page 22.

Peanuts: Not really a nut at all, but rather a type of legume that grows underground, peanuts are seeds nestled inside waffle-veined pods that become thin and brittle when dried.

Pecans: The pecan has two deeply crinkled lobes of nutmeat, much like its relative, the walnut. All pecans have smooth, brown oval shells that break easily and a sweet delicate flavor.

Pistachios: Pistachios have creamy tan, thin, hard, rounded outer shells. As the nuts ripen, their shells crack to reveal light green kernels.

POTATOES

Red: Also known simply as boiling or all-purpose potatoes, red potatoes have a thin red skin and a waxy flesh that keeps its shape, making them excellent for roasting and boiling.

Russet: Also known as baking potatoes, russet potatoes are large and oval, with dry, reddish brown skin. Their starchy flesh is perfect for baking and mashing.

Yukon Gold: Thin-skinned potatoes with yellowish skin and golden, fine-grained, buttery-tasting flesh. These all-purpose potatoes hold their shape when boiled, and they make colorful mashed potatoes as well.

SEEDS

Sesame: These tiny, flat seeds are available in brown, red, and black varieties, but the most common sesame seeds are a pale tan. They add a nutty flavor to any food and are often sprinkled over savory dishes as a garnish.

Sunflower: Harvested from the large, dark centers of bright yellow sunflowers, these seeds have hard black-and-white-striped shells. The shells are removed to reveal small, slightly sweet seeds. These seeds are valued for the cooking oil they yield and are a popular snack food.

SHALLOTS Small members of the onion family, shallots have brownish skin and white flesh tinged with purple. Their flavor is a cross between sweet onion and garlic, and they are often used in recipes that would be overpowered by the stronger taste of onions.

SHORTENING, VEGETABLE Solid vegetable fat made by hydrogenating a vegetable oil, such as cottonseed or soybean. Shortening contains millions of tiny air bubbles and so requires less creaming than butter and makes tender, light-textured baked goods. Because it is virtually flavorless, shortening is some-times used in place of, or in combination with, butter.

SHRIMP, DEVEINING Some shrimp (prawns) have a dark intestinal vein running through them that is removed primarily for aesthetic reasons. Shrimp deveining gadgets can be used, but a paring knife does the job just fine. Make a shallow cut following the curve of the back of the shrimp just down to the vein. Slip the tip of the knife under the vein, lift it, pull the vein away, and rinse the shrimp under cold water.

STOCK A flavorful liquid derived from slowly simmering chicken, meat, fish, or vegetables in water, along with herbs and aromatic ingredients such as onions. Stock can be made easily at home and frozen for future use. Good-quality canned broths are also available, but they tend to be saltier than homemade stock, so seek out those labeled "low-sodium" to most effectively control the flavoring in your dish.

SWEET POTATOES Not true potatoes, although resembling them in form, these tuberous vegetables have light brown skin and pale yellow flesh. Sweet potatoes are prized for their natural sweetness when cooked. (See also page 89.)

TRUSSING PINS Flexible metal pins with hooked ends, used to close up the cavity of poultry before roasting. The pins are inserted across a stuffed cavity and kitchen string is used to lace the opening closed. (For more details, see page 112.)

VINEGAR

Balsamic: Balsamic vinegar is a specialty of the Italian region of Emilia-Romagna, primarily the town of Modena. It is made from white Trebbiano grapes and is long aged in wooden casks, which contributes to its final flavor. Labeled *aceto balsamico tradizionale,* true balsamic vinegar must be aged for at least 12 years (but often sits much longer). It is prized for its rich and intense flavor.

Cider: Made from apples, cider vinegar is used in many traditional American recipes and is noted for its distinctive apple flavor.

Red Wine: Produced when wine is fermented for a second time, red wine vinegar is sharply acidic. The vinegar, like the wine from which it is made, has a more robust flavor than vinegar produced from white wine.

Sherry: Of Spanish origin, sherry vinegar has a nutty taste and is especially good with vegetables and in dressings.

WATERCRESS This member of the mustard family has small, round, dark green leaves on short, delicate stems. Watercress has a refreshing, peppery flavor that turns bitter with age. It grows wild along streams and is cultivated in water. When preparing watercress, rinse the sprigs carefully to remove any trace of dirt. Pick over the sprigs, choosing only the freshest leaves and discarding any that are yellow or wilted. Remove and discard the thick stems as well.

INDEX

SIMON & SCHUSTER SOURCE
A Division of Simon & Schuster
Rockefeller Center, 1230 Avenue of the Americas,
New York, NY 10020

WILLIAMS-SONOMA
Founder and Vice-Chairman: Chuck Williams
Book Buyer: Cecilia Michaelis

WELDON OWEN INC.
Chief Executive Officer: John Owen
President: Terry Newell
Chief Operating Officer: Larry Partington
Vice President, International Sales: Stuart Laurence
Creative Director: Gaye Allen
Series Editor: Sarah Putman Clegg
Associate Editor: Heather Belt
Copy Editor: Carolyn Miller
Consulting Editor: Sharon Silva
Designer: Douglas Chalk
Production Manager: Chris Hemesath
Production Assistant: Donita Boles
Studio Manager: Brynn Breuner
Production Designer: Joan Olson
Photograph Editor: Lisa Lee
Food Photographer: Noel Barnhurst
Food Stylist: Sandra Cook
Indexer: Ken DellaPenta
Proofreaders: Desne Border, Ken DellaPenta,
Kate Chynoweth, Linda Bouchard,
Arin Hailey, Carrie Bradley

Williams-Sonoma Collection *Thanksgiving* was
conceived and produced by Weldon Owen Inc.,
814 Montgomery Street, San Francisco,
California 94133, in collaboration with
Williams-Sonoma, 3250 Van Ness Avenue,
San Francisco, California 94109.

A Weldon Owen Production
Copyright © 2001 by Weldon Owen Inc. and
Williams-Sonoma Inc.

Set in Trajan, Utopia, and Vectora.

Color separations by Bright Arts Graphics
Singapore (Pte.) Ltd.
Printed and bound in Singapore by Tien Wah
Press (Pte.) Ltd.

First printed in 2001.

10 9 8 7 6 5 4 3 2

Library of Congress Cataloging-in-Publication
Data is available.

ISBN 0-7432-2502-3

A NOTE ON WEIGHTS AND MEASURES

All recipes include customary U.S. and metric measurements. Metric conversions are based on
a standard developed for these books and have been rounded off. Actual weights may vary.